2001

NOTES BY A NOMAD

To Oliver & Jane who received the postcards.

Craig

NOTES BY A NOMAD

Travel Stories

Craig Dixon

Copyright © 2001 by Craig Dixon.

ISBN #: Softcover 1-4010-1334-1
Library of Congress Number: 2001117355

All rights reserved. No part of this book may be reproduced or transmitted in any form or by any means, electronic or mechanical, including photocopying, recording, or by any information storage and retrieval system, without permission in writing from the copyright owner.

This is a work of non fiction but the names of several people and institutions in several stories have been changed. The author apologizes for, and does not hold himself responsible for, any statistical errors or inadvertent misrepresentations of business circumstances.

This book was printed in the United States of America.

To order additional copies of this book, contact:
Xlibris Corporation
1-888-795-4274
www.Xlibris.com
Orders@Xlibris.com

CONTENTS

Rhapsody 9

Back to Bucharest 11

Eight Hours Are Barely Enough. 21

National Pride 29

A Day in the Andes 31

An Introduction to Trickle Up 36

Trickle Up goes to Tonga 37

South India Startups 40

My Industrial-Strength Summer 48

Thai Tale 69

Kiwi Kindness 72

Foot by Foot across England 79

To my wife Rosy, and my daughter Andrea, with love.

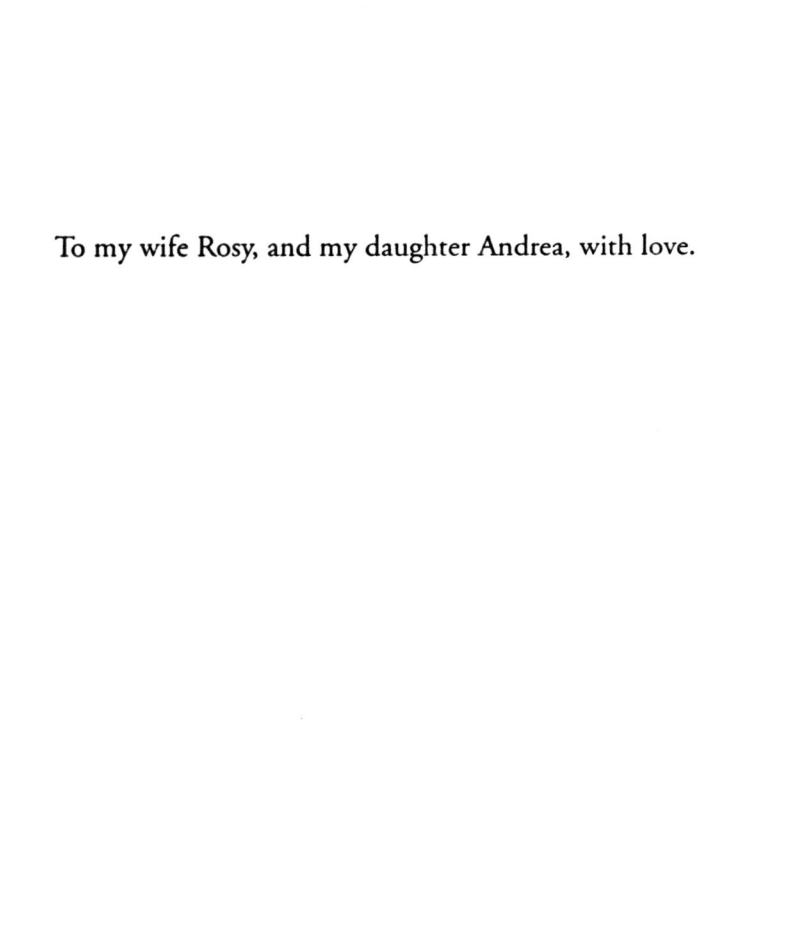

RHAPSODY

The musician sat on a low stool in the middle of a large lawn outside the Royal Palace on Castle Hill in Buda, across the river from Pest. She was wearing an orange wool cap, a blue ski jacket, a flowing, red paisley skirt and combat boots. A plastic shopping bag lay near her left foot.

"Is she singing in Hungarian or German?" my wife asked me.

"No idea." I shrugged my shoulders.

We were sitting on a bench, taking a cigarette break from sightseeing, and it was pleasant to be entertained in the cool Hungarian spring sunshine by a colorful guitarist. She didn't look up at all from her instrument, and she sang one mournful song after another in a quavery voice.

The guitarist was sitting about fifty feet away from us and the tourists were streaming from the Palace to the funicular station. By her isolation she seemed to be making her own artistic statement rather than operating a commercial endeavor.

I started imagining her frugal but independent life. Possibly she was an Esterhazy or a Habsburg whose recent ancestors had lost everything under one of the totalitarian governments. Or maybe she supported her father, a retired professor of music ethnography. He'd been her teacher, and he blithely thought that she put goulash on the table from a job she'd told him she had in computer programming.

"Somebody ought to teach her about body language and rapport with her target market." I've been a salesman all my life.

Whatever the musician's history she now seemed wrapped up in herself, and too far away to be working the crowd. Yet from where we were sitting she looked poorly dressed enough to show need. I wanted to take a photo of her with my new zoom lens. The lone, multicolored figure against the lush green lawn with the grey Palace behind her looked like a good composition through my viewfinder.

"Don't you dare." My wife is big on human rights.

"Why not?"

"It doesn't seem right."

"I don't really think that I'm invading her privacy. It's public land here."

I picked a moment to aim the camera when my subject was particularly intent on her guitar. Then it was time to head off to catch the funicular down to the Danube.

"I want to give her money." I said.

"To pay for the sneaky photo, huh? I bet she won't take it," my wife retorted.

But to show solidarity or to check up on her wager, my wife walked across the lawn with me. The nearer we came to the musician the more hawklike her features appeared. She didn't stop playing as we approached and I noticed that her jacket was quite ragged. On her guitar case there were several coins, but they weren't visible until you were close to her. I added some to them and then I felt entitled to give her advice.

Assuming that she was Hungarian with their impenetrable language, I made what I hoped was a clear physical gesture. By moving both my arms laterally in front of me and making wave motions, I indicated that she should move her operation nearer to the pathway, where the action was. She paused in her playing and looked us up and down.

In perfect unaccented English she said, "But you paid anyway."

BACK TO BUCHAREST

The airport terminal has been gutted and mostly refurbished, with Italian money I'm told. And as you taxi to the terminal, there's still the row of cannibalized Tarom jets, so I guess that the aid package hasn't yet extended to a maintenance hangar or a parts warehouse.

The passport officers have computers instead of greasy ledgers. The baggage carousel creaks, but it works. There are bright yellow Camel ashtrays all over the place. In the entrance to the restroom there's a roll of toilet paper, and now in 1995, nobody's guarding it. But the seats for the toilets, which were ordered in 1992, haven't arrived as yet.

I'm here for a conference. The subject is Economic Restructuring — a staple and stale topic in Bucharest now for the last five years. I'd helped establish a Romanian Raw Materials Exchange in 1992 for an aid agency, and the Exchange sponsored this 1995 conference, with generous help from Reuters. The Exchange does business now for just two hours, one day a week, so Reuters is a truly farsighted missionary. But I'm sure that their people are aware that Romania is the size of Oregon, and it has a population 8% that of the United States.

The economy is still over 80% government-owned, and the state-run companies don't feel any urgent need to use the Exchange. Still, those two hours of transactions represent real progress. Back in 1992 we were writing the rules of the Exchange at the very same time that the government was drafting the national commercial code.

In my training classes then, I'd had to explain to the young prospective brokerage personnel that profits had to be earned.

They'd assumed that profits were just handed out. Many thought that profits would be distributed like the company share vouchers that the whole population received in the early 1990's. That had been a pre-privatization program; an initiative developed by the government elected after 'President for Life' Ceausescu was mercifully gunned down on Christmas Day, 1989.

Much of the discussion at the conference is about an imminent privatization law. When that's passed and Romania has some companies with real shareholders, then they'll tackle the establishment of a stock exchange. For the moment, they only have the Raw Material Exchange, which only trades...raw materials. One of the frustrations Romanian people have felt is that there's been nowhere to cash in or trade all the company vouchers they were given — except with the Gypsies who set up shop outside the central railroad station. Yes, indeed, Gypsies are the first stockbrokers of Romania!

Because the mad dictator had such a tight grip on the people until his death, there was no extensive Mafia to become the entrepreneurs in the new freer economy, the way it has in Russia. Sure, the Securitate police had business dealings, but they haven't been able to surface too obviously in the '90s. But from time immemorial there have been Gypsies. Ceaucescu's border controls made them less nomadic, more settled and urban, but still undocumented and fiercely independent. But now a few of them are driving BMWs and hiring English tutors.

By the way, Romanians get upset over three misconceptions about them as a people—that they're all Slavs, Gypsies or vampires.

When I was here in 1992 people looked Slavic to me, suspicious and closed-faced. To say that they look less Slavic now, is to forget that this is a Latin country. It was the easternmost province of the Roman Empire, and its language is written in the same alphabet as ours, and looks somewhat like Esperanto. Anyone with basic French, Spanish or Italian can generally figure out what people are talking about, or what the subject is on a page of print. So Romeania is not Slav at all.

The Gypsies are all over the place. That's for sure. They operate most of the fruit and vegetable markets, and their kids are a nuisance on the streets. After Ceausescu, when the mass migrations occurred, particularly into Germany, the looks of Romanian asylum seekers were so saturnine or Latinate that the blond Germans regarded them all as Gypsies. But this Roma group, as they are called, is officially only one or two percent of the population.

Romania, with its province of Transylvania, is not the country of the fictional Dracula. Bram Stoker never came here. He spent his life in the British Isles, and he based the vampire's castle on one he saw in Scotland. But it's a great story.

In 1992 if you expressed interest in the subject you might be able to arrange a visit to Bran Castle which looks like a vampire might have lived there. It's actually only an old provincial customs post. But now you can buy Bloodcount vodka, fiery Transylvanian Tzuica brandy and Dracula dolls there. The locals now only giggle when you make vampire jokes, but three years ago they were shocked if you denigrated the original Dracul/Prince, Vlad Tepes, the Great Impaler, who freed them from the Turks. The dripping blood on ancient German lithographs of Prince Vlad's exploits inspired Bram Stoker, and he invented the tale that has so distorted the popular perception of this area.

People *do* look different now. In 1992, only some of the rich-looking women in the capital city center wore western fashions. Makeup was often glaringly multicolored around their big brown eyes. Many hair hues and styles looked extra-terrestrial. Since then, the cosmetic companies have sent in their teams of trainers and they've set up direct selling networks. Now, most women show that they know how to attract, with the latest fashions and beauty aids.

Men are still formal, but they're wearing better suits. They have smarter eyeglasses too, and their ties are of a more up-to-date width. Stylish haircuts are common, but men's shoes still seem to be a holdout. They're plastic looking, clunky old designs. There is some sort of male sartorial foot-dragging going on.

The Hotel Dorobanti has deteriorated. In 1992 I was here for the whole month of June, so I really got a sense of the place. Fortunately, this visit is only for a week. In 1992, the water supply was sporadic, now it's the electricity that you can't count on. There are better hotels in Bucharest, and more of them now, but this is my place. It's the one that the agency will pay for.

When I arrive this time, accompanied by the Reuters people, a room can't be assigned to me. We're late for a Welcome cocktail party. It's the first of many, followed by at least as many Farewell ones. After signing the registration card I hand off my bag to the concierge and go off to the Reuters festivities. When I come back to the hotel after dinner, a room has been assigned to me, but there's no bag in it. A phone call to reception brings a smiling serf, with the wrong bag. I describe mine, write my name in block letters for him, and he brings the right-colored bag, but with no tag, and anyway it isn't mine. He requests me to come visit the storage cellar, which also doesn't contain my bag, and finally he finds it under the reception desk, directly below the phone he had been using when he'd talked to me.

Just as in 1992, a high level of intelligence is not a prerequisite for working at the Dorobanti. In fact, I find out that diligence and innovation are actually frowned on, for good reason. When the hotel is privatized and sold, the management will be allowed to buy shares, and they want to make sure that the shares will be cheap. It's a good example of the problems of progression in this part of the world. They're going from everyone owning everything, to anyone being permitted to buy anything if money is available.

The room I have is smaller than the one I had last time. I'm particularly conscious of that in the design of the entrance area. Doors open against other doors. It would be difficult even for a small, agile person to move around without risk of injury. Checking out the bathroom, I find that now there's toilet paper actually in place, not just provided on request by the floor concierge. But there's a lock on the paper container, and Romanians make some of the best locks in the world.

The color scheme is the same as in my old 1992 room. In fact, it's the same color scheme I've seen in every state run Eastern Bloc hotel I've ever stayed in — bilious green walls, puke orange upholstery and varnished blond wood. But the sheets have been changed. Back in 1992 I suffered starched, stiff, square damask tablecloths on the bed, but now I have soft, rectangular, plain cotton bedsheets.

The huge satellite dish on the roof of the hotel is an indication that mine is not the only room with a TV. In 1992 a TV was installed in my room for me in return for a carton of Marlboros donated to the floor matron who had seed pearls sewn all over her tight pink sweater. She's moved on, as have the floor maids who'd offered me "Little Scotty" whisky at 8 am and were snoring drunk on my bed with the TV blaring when I'd come back at lunchtime. Now, three years later, there are so many overseas channels that I ration my television intake so as not to distort my sense of being in a foreign place.

This room has a balcony. In the heat of June 1992 I could have used one, but at least this room is not over the nightclub, which even in 1992 was going all night, most nights of the week. The beat still throbs down there, but now there's competition from clubs all over town.

This time I've got a good view of Ceausescu's newer part of the city. There's the Peoples Palace that's second in size to the Pentagon, and the avenues of apartments with a dozen rusty cranes over the still unfinished sections. One, very privileged architect did the whole project. There's no money to take away the cranes, or finish the apartments and no one's decided what to do with the Palace. Even now, foreigners seem to be the only people who talk about it. Romanians are still too conscious of the privations they suffered while so many resources were squandered on it. I have to admit that its proportions seem less weird the second time around, or perhaps it's the effect of the evergreens that have grown up around the perimeter.

As it's winter during this visit, I don't linger on the hotel balcony, but I'm aware that through the bare deciduous tree branches, one sees much more of the architectural details of the city, the romantic turrets on the villas, and the Habsburg or Parisian scale of the central public buildings.

Looking down into the street, I don't see the used light bulb man displaying his wares. He used to stand at the bus stop every day and I guess he's no longer in business. His market niche intrigued me when I was here in 1992. The people I worked with explained the process to me. Because of the shortages, you would buy a dead bulb from him, take it to the office and insert it into a socket. Then you'd claim a replacement from the building maintenance, and you'd have a good light bulb to take home to the family. Now, light bulbs are prominently displayed in a number of shop windows, and looking out from the balcony at night, the newly illuminated buildings give sparkling magic and majesty to the city.

Like so many other things in the hotel, the elevators haven't been fixed. But in three years I've forgotten that I should take something to read while waiting for them. When I was here before I once got so exasperated that I walked down the emergency stairs nine flights, only to find that the door out to the lobby was locked, and if someone out there heard me banging on it, he certainly didn't care.

A pleasant surprise awaits me when I come down to breakfast this time. There are no moneychangers waiting in the corridor to the restaurant with their wads of counterfeit bills. These days, many shops have a government approved currency exchange kiosk in them. But the street guys have developed some new scams. A couple of days later I experience one.

It was on a crowded, shopping street and I wasn't much surprised when a currency trader in black leather hissed at me. "I give you some good rate! Better than kiosk, more lei for your dollars, also D-marks". He was trotting along beside me.

I didn't need any lei as the Agency had given me walking around money. But I always enjoy the haggling process and I tried to work him up to a ridiculously favorable rate. When he realized I wasn't a real prospect he fell back into the crowd. Seconds later, two large men in formal overcoats grabbed my arms and barked, "Police! You must give us your passport now! You do criminal money change. We take you jail!"

I'd heard some chat at the hotel about the phony police shakedowns, so I was mildly suspicious of them. But I have to admit I was emboldened in my protests by the sight of the gold ring in the ear of one of them. When I told them in English to piss off, remarkably they did.

The blind people are still working in the massage salon at the municipal spa. The price has gone up since 1992 to 7000 lei ($3.50). I can be a big spender with five dollars. There's a change in routine though. The blind lady masseuse now wants me to keep my shorts on during the massage. It's not a new prudish phase, but these days she finds a need to differentiate herself from the sighted unlicensed lascivious ladies operating down the street. Strident Rom-Rap is now playing through the spa Musak system. The masseuse says that she likes the rhythm better than the old folkloric music that was on the government station. Her technique reflects the musical change of pace though, so I only visit the spa once on this trip.

Gelu still lives in Bangladesh. That's what the taxi driver calls Gelu's neighborhood when I go out there to visit this time around. There isn't much that can be called infrastructure in that part of the city, just row after row of apartment complexes that were built in the '70s but never properly finished. And neighborliness is not much in evidence. When we get lost in the dark, and nobody will help, the taxi driver seems to be cursing himself for giving me a fixed rate.

In 1992 I'd been asked by Gelu's ex-wife Emilia in New York to deliver some cash to Gelu and his ailing mother. He'd had to stay in Bucharest to look after her. Back then, when he'd opened the door of the apartment, he'd glared at me and started practicing his newly acquired English.

"Are you fucking her? Had you fucked? Will you fuck her?"

He'd cheered up somewhat when I told him that I only knew his ex-wife from my workplace. I congratulated him on his grasp of English conjugation and gave him what I'd brought him from America. He thanked me profusely, particularly when he found that the money envelope included pictures of his daughter, then twelve years old. That Sunday I was guest of honor at his party, with lots of his art college friends, chain smoking, with the fiery tuica flowing.

Gelu had said, "Help yourself to food. Our tradition is that you eat until you are ashamed of yourself." This didn't take long, because sadly, there wasn't much on the table.

This was less than two years after a total ban on even speaking with foreigners, and at that time I must have seemed like a curiosity from another planet. My eyes were stared into, my hands gripped and squeezed. I was kissed by all and sundry, and I developed a razor burn rash. The abyss between our lifestyles was so wide that they seemed not to know what favors to ask of me. There was an implication that henceforth I would be their connection either to a better life in the West or to things brought from the West.

In fact, Emilia was the Western connection, but reluctantly. In 1992 she'd written to the family in advance and I was expected. This time she told me that her Romanian family's economic expectations had been raised very high.

"Please," she said guiltily, "just give them the envelope, keep the taxi waiting outside, and pretend to be in a hurry."

Now, I was thinking about what she'd said. On the long drive out there I debated with myself whether I'd satisfy my curiosity and again accept a Sunday invitation to a feast. The taxi driver was giving me his perspective on present day life in Bucharest. He spoke perfect French, and that reminded me of the French-speaking drivers I'd had three years before.

In 1992 it had been a nightmare of a ride out to Gelu's neighborhood. I'd ridden in a clapped out Dacia, the locally built Renault knockoff. Two drivers had been necessary to operate the vehicle, one to crank it and the other to pump the gas pedal. When we'd got going, the co-driver had had to hold the passenger door closed with one hand, and steady the rearview mirror with the other. There were no outside mirrors. I'd started counting how many normal car attributes the taxi lacked, and I remembered that the only indication of its taxi status had been a cardboard sign in the window. When we got out to Gelu's building, the driver had tried to get 80,000 lei ($40). He claimed in French that he'd forgotten to say "quatre-vingt" instead of "quatre". It was a good try, quite a creative use of his second language really, but I was glad that I didn't need him further. Fortunately Emilia had assured me that the family would get me back to the city center. Gelu told me that $10 was ample for the taxi.

Now I'm riding in a brand new Toyota Camry, part of a well-advertised fleet of cabs. It has a powerful citrus air freshener and an efficiently ticking meter. The rate seems pleasantly cheap, until the driver informs me, in the middle of Bangladesh, that a zero will be added to the fare. Out here where I trust him to wait for me, I have to believe him, or walk, or depend on Gelu and his family

As I stand in the smelly, ratty stairwell, pressing the bell on Gelu's graffiti covered door, I decide that I really prefer the false international atmosphere of the central city, where nothing personal is expected of me, just business. I don't want to bring more stress back to Emilia in New York or raise expectations here. Progress is polarizing, that's for sure. When the door opens, I breathe out, repelling the fetid heat and cigarette fumes. I'd smoked heavily in 1992 and now I was trying to stop. I complete my task and make my profuse pathetic excuses to Gelu. We manage an awkward hug, and I'm off with the patient cab driver.

The conference is over and I'll be flying home tomorrow. During my last night of my visit, the Dorobanti room phone wakes me up about once an hour, and each time the switchboard woman insists that my phone could not have rung. But it does ring, loudly. I can even hear it start to ring again at 6 am, as I shoulder my bag and close the door behind me.

At the airport I find that I have plenty of time to explore as the plane is delayed for de-icing. The gift shop sells Dracula slivovitz with a red label. Palinka, the other local firewater, has been upgraded from plastic screw top bottles to ceramic flasks, with ribbons on the neck and multicolored embossed labels.

The business class lounge (which didn't exist in 1992) has all the normal 1995 accoutrements. A special local touch, however, is a glass-walled tropical area filled with plastic flora and yellow patio furniture. There's a tinkling, winding stream with an arched Japanese bridge over it, and a lighted waterfall. They must be planning for wedding receptions or maybe a tanning salon.

As I turn and look back from the steps up to the plane, I notice that, above the terminal, there's only one letter unlit in the Bucharest name sign. Next time, who knows, total illumination? I'm not sure that I look forward to seeing it any time soon.

EIGHT HOURS ARE BARELY ENOUGH.

"I want to try out that theory of mine about using the air conditioner as a soothing white noise," Rosy said. She was slipping on her long tee shirt for the night ahead.

"Yes, darling," I countered. "But that means that I'll have to simultaneously test *my* theory about how much heat the human body needs for survival."

I was already searching the hotel room closet for extra blankets. During our long marriage we've actually agreed about several things, but the ideal bedroom temperature is not one of them.

We were on vacation in Portugal, and by the third day there was an issue between us. We could nervously joke about it, but only in the afternoons. What disturbance would wake Rosy up? At the next hotel, what would arouse her from slumber before her optimal wake up time?

How do I know what her optimal wake up time is? If I've gone to sleep before her, which I inevitably do, then I don't know when she started her eight hours. So far our morning conversations had been limited strictly to the logistics of travel.

The first night of the vacation, we'd been in Lisbon with all the usual big city traffic noises. A back room didn't help. Everything echoed through the airshaft outside our window. Also, we had to contend with jet lag after a delayed and uncomfortable flight. We use eye shades and neck pillows on airplanes, but not earplugs. Some years before, on a noisy crowded train in India we'd both tried wax plugs. We'd each rammed them in so hard that our hearing was affected for days. We'd had to use sign language and read lips.

It hadn't made much difference in terms of our contact with the natives, but with each other it was a bit weird.

Rosy is an ideal travel companion as long as we have a car, and no reservations beyond the first night. Public transport schedules are problematic and I sweat plane departure times, though she tells me I don't need to. We have different sleep needs. I thrive on five or six hours, but Rosy needs at least two or three more. I fall back to sleep easily after being disturbed, she doesn't. We have different body clocks. At home, we move quietly around each other's rest patterns. On vacation, the daily schedules of travelling bring about some uncomfortable synchronization.

Setting off from Lisbon towards northern Portugal, Rosy slept fitfully in our rented car. I explored two monasteries, a ducal palace and a royal library. After two thousand years of active clerics and kings, these institutions are thick on the ground there. We zigzagged our way through history.

That night we stayed in Obidos. It's the hill village whose bougainvillea-draped walls are featured in the tourist ads for Portugal. The streets are so narrow that the side mirrors on our car grazed the house walls on both sides. The village is drop-dead gorgeous, and as we were travelling in October it was blissfully cool and quiet up there. We'd wanted to stay in the government sponsored pousada deep inside Obidos castle, but it was full. The manager made a phone call for us though and we were fixed up at a delightful traditional house below the castle walls. The window of the tastefully decorated room was set in a wall three feet thick, and we had a view of the twinkling lights of the valley below.

"I'll bet they call this place Albuergo Overflow. The castle is probably booked up solid most nights." I hung up a clean shirt for the morning.

"I'm happy for them. We've got a cozy little room here anyway, and it's sooo quiet." Rosy started humming as she unpacked her clothes.

"Most of the houses in this village must be owned by Germans,

Swedes and Brits. Just people who only come here on vacation." It seemed to me the only reason for the silence of the place.

"I know I'll sleep well here, I just feel it," said Rosy, "and God knows, I need it."

I can't remember which started first, the dogs or the roosters, but by 6am they were all creating a symphony which was gradually replaced by the sound of the tourists' cars coming out of the gates of the castle. First, we heard the splat-splat of the tires on the cobblestones as the vehicles came down the slope towards the house. Then, rubber squealing, they made the tight turn through the tiny square. The final orchestral movement was the grinding of their gears as the cars faced the hill up to the church, and down again out to the main road.

Another breakfast without grace and the happy banter of carefree vacationing.

"You know, don't you, that I don't blame the creatures themselves when I curse at the dogs." Rosy looked intently at me. "It's their owners I'd like to murder. They just don't control or train the poor things."

I saved a childhood story to tell her later. On the farm where my family went for vacation I once took a big flashlight out to the hen house at three in the morning to fool the rooster into crowing. I couldn't believe my effectiveness, so I made the rooster crow several mornings in a row. Then I was caught and punished for rousing the household prematurely.

That afternoon, we had a splendid time exploring a gastronomic festival in Santarem. We wandered past stalls carrying all kinds of delicacies we never managed to find on restaurant menus.

Rosy whispered to me, "Look at his cute little crescent of bald patch." She nodded towards an old man wearing farm boots walking in front of us. A small battered snap-brim hat was pushed forward on his big head.

"Do you think his parents bought the hat for him when he was little?"

"Yeah, something like that," I grinned. "One hat per lifetime."

Then we headed out to the Atlantic coast.

In Aveiro, the Venice of Portugal, I didn't trust my language skills so I mimed to explain Rosy's needs to the manager of the Hotel Montejo. He gave me a long-suffering look.

"There are no cockerels, canines or truck routes, sir, in the area surrounding our hotel." he assured me in perfect, plummy English. "Madam will sleep soundly here."

I reflected that if he were a true Brit he would have said 'lorry' instead of 'truck', and it comforted me that he felt a pandering need to adapt his language for us Yanks. Well, Rosy is a born and bred American and I've lived there long enough to qualify as a superior being.

We strolled through the old town and looked at the menus outside the restaurants. As in other towns, without exception, the codfish section was three times as long as that of the meat.

"If we stay in this country too long, I'll grow fins," Rosy said. "They really love their bacalao."

A couple of blocks from the hotel a neighborhood Saturday night fiesta was in progress. There was a small town travelling carnival, bumper cars, cotton candy and a rickety old carousel. Kids of all ages, boisterous, but not at all rowdy. A sad eyed man in costume was singing fado.

Rosy said, "I wish we knew the words."

I nodded, "Think of the country and western songs you know, and strip out all the references to modern things like trucks and TV."

We enjoyed the local scene for a while, then we turned in. The hotel manager told us that the carnival would close down at midnight. "It's sponsored by the Church, and they want everyone to be able to get up for Mass."

The sea air smelled wonderful through our open window.

At 7am, we thought war had broken out. Gunfire! It was unmistakable but measured in its frequency. The shooting ended after about fifteen minutes.

"What the hell was that?" Rosy was sitting bolt upright.

"I think I've just figured out what that sign was that we saw around the corner last night. It said Campo do Tiror. And I'll bet we've just heard some idiot practicing for a clay pigeon shoot."

"Terrific." Rosy was burrowing under her pillow, and she'd just started gently snoring again, when church bells all over town reminded us that the parishioners were being called to worship.

After breakfast, we dozed on a warm wall by the estuary, waiting for a boat that was supposed to tour the canals of the delta. Rosy was stroking a stray kitten.

"What a little fur ball. Such an uncomplicated life. I want to come back as a cat."

After a while I suggested that we give up on waiting for the boatman.

"Maybe he was injured in the morning clay shoot," Rosy muttered. We walked off to the car park.

She was completely awake when we got to the shrine of Fatima. I suggested that she visit the holy place on her knees. She could pray for a good night's sleep.

The Fatima shrine is where three peasant children, tending their sheep, saw the Blessed Virgin Mary in 1917. Even though the anniversary had passed a couple of weeks before, I pointed out that there were still a couple of dozen crawling penitents who would keep her company along the way.

She laughed, and it made my day.

By that evening we'd driven up to Vaina do Costelo, north of Oporto, and here we seriously researched the local hotel situation. There's a basilica, called Santa Luzia, way above the city, on a rocky outcrop in a forest. It's a popular Sunday picnic spot, and above the basilica, set in its own private gardens, there's a hotel with the same name. It's posh, expensive, and secluded. The only road for miles around is the road that leads to it. And, glory be, we seemed to be the only guests at the hotel that night.

Here I didn't try to do my mime. The reception clerk who greeted us turned out to have just arrived that week. He hailed from Paterson, New Jersey.

"Oh, you won't have any problems like that here," he said, after hearing Rosy's tale of woe. "I've slept like a baby every night since Monday, when I started here." He thought that hunting was probably prohibited in the forest.

He'd grown up in a Portuguese immigrant family, and was planning to check out his roots here for a while.

"After Paterson, I find this place a bit too quiet and secluded, but I've committed to the hotel for six months. Then, we'll see how it goes."

The room was lovely. The bathroom, set inside a small vestibule, had walls of delicately figured marble. Like the lobby downstairs, the room was done in art deco style throughout, as the hotel had been built in the Twenties. Beyond the beds, French doors opened onto a wide flower-filled balcony, overlooking the basilica and the Douro River estuary beyond. The picnickers below had mostly gone home, and we'd checked with the desk that there was no Monday morning Mass scheduled.

As we were the only guests I was sure that housekeeping activities wouldn't start early. But, as usual, I hung out Rosy's custom designed "DO NOT DISTURB" sign that is boldly printed in ten languages. The temperature was ideal so there was no need for a noisy air conditioner. It had been a sunny day. The air was mild and pine scented. We could sleep with the balcony doors wide open.

We found CNN International on the television and I nodded off during a program about Mozambique.

Two dogs started yapping at around 2am. They were loud and clear and I imagined that I knew what they looked like. Terrier types probably, small and hyperactive, stupid from centuries of in-breeding. My first thought was that whatever they were, they'd been roused by a late car on the hill, and that they'd soon stop.

Twenty minutes later, Rosy got up, and closed the windows and fire shutters, trailing a stream of invective.

"This is ridiculous, darling." I gently protested, "Now we'll get no air."

But the sound of the dogs still penetrated and she phoned the desk.

"I don't know who the hell is responsible for those dogs, but, Christ, you've got to do something." There was a pause while she listened.

"All right then, good night."

"Was it the guy from Paterson you talked to?" I asked.

"No, a local. He says he'll do what he can."

But the yapping continued, as if the dogs were barking directly at each other. A canine territorial dispute in deepest, darkest Portugal.

Rosy groaned, and reached over me.

"What's happening?" She shouted into the phone. "Did you do *anything*? With the money we're paying for this room, we're entitled to some peace and quiet. Don't they have ordinances against this kind of noise?"

I suppressed an unkind giggle that her use of the word 'ordinances' threatened to generate.

"Oh, really!" Rosy seemed to have reached an impasse with whomever she was talking to on the phone. "Oh! So that means that you can't do a damn thing. And they own all the land around you, huh? Shit!" and she banged down the phone.

"The fucking dogs belong to the Church!"

She grabbed some of the bedding and a pillow.

Announcing to the world, "This'll do it," she stomped into the vestibule closing the connecting door firmly behind her.

I drifted off to sleep, thinking about the stone-deaf priests. How did they handle whispered confessions?

When I awoke, early as usual, Rosy was nowhere to be seen, but the connecting door was closed and I assumed that she was still sacked out on the floor beyond it. Now, I couldn't get to the bathroom. Desperate, I took a leak in the flowerbed on the balcony, and then I read the guide books till she surfaced. There was no sound now from the dogs.

Over breakfast, the American employee from New Jersey came

by our table to chat. He'd heard the dogs too, and he'd asked the waiters about them.

"The only connection the Church has," he informed us, "is that the picnickers hope that the priests in their kindness, will look after the dogs. On Sundays, the men in some families get so fed up at home with the barking of their dogs that they bring the critters up with the family for a picnic. Then they 'lose' them. Those two dogs we heard last night were probably tied to trees in the woods. That way they wouldn't follow the men back. The waiters told me that it happens most often in the fall, when these guys contemplate being indoors more during the winter months."

Rosy was mortified.

"Oh, no!" She wailed, "How could I have cursed those poor little creatures, alone and hungry, tied up and frightened in the forest. I wonder what happened to them. It's so unfair."

She made the clerk promise to search out and feed the dogs. Then, we set off back towards Lisbon. I know that her pain was compounded by the thought that there was no practical way she could do anything more for them.

NATIONAL PRIDE

The railway inspector caught me. It was on the mid-morning train from La Spezia to Genoa. My destination was Pavia where I would be meeting Luigi's family. The connection that I'd have to make at Genoa was a tight one. I'd be racing between platforms.

"You must pay a supplement." The inspector's face looked like a kneecap, meaty and mottled.

"Why? No one told me when I bought the ticket." My Italian is patchy so I was embellishing the words with gestures. It probably looked something like semaphore, with the flags.

I looked vainly for support to the two Italian ladies sitting opposite me. They'd already shown their tickets without incident. The older one pursed her lips and concentrated on her book. The other one had been looking at me with curiosity until I tried to engage her sympathy by raising my eyebrows. Instantly she found something fascinating to stare at out the train window.

"This train is a Rapido. You must pay extra for that." Peering at his rate book, the inspector didn't bother looking at me. He probably had to check the whole train before the next station.

"But it's running late, it's not a Rapido at the moment." I smiled up at him slyly.

"Signore," he shrugged and glanced at his watch and tapped his book. "My regulations are clear." Now he was looking at me. There was a confident light in his eyes. I would pay and he would have the last word.

"That will be twenty nine thousand lire. You will be able to make your connection without a problem at Genoa. We will certainly make up the lost time. The Italian Rapido service always recovers *any* lost time... unlike your own trains over there in the United States of America."

A DAY IN THE ANDES

On the way from Caracas to Merida the plane lands somewhere to wait for the fog to lift. Merida lies in a high narrow trench between two mountains. This is the northern end of the Andes. All the other airlines, other than mine, use smaller planes. They can land in the fog.

In Merida, I'm met by Jerry, the local adventure tour operator, supporter of Chavez and computer entrepreneur. He's an Anglophile whose birth name is Jerome, which he uses for all formal salutations. It reminds me that I used to work with a Jerry/Jerome stockbroker whose assistant always had to formally announce him on the phone as Jerome.

My Venezuelan guide for the mountains is Jefferson L. Gonzalez. He's slightly hyper, with very intense eyes. We'll get into his name later. We rearrange backpacks at Jerry's office. I'd assumed mules were to be used, but it seems that I have to carry my stuff for the four day trip. Jefferson can't help me because he's lugging food and emergency stuff for the two of us.

Now we board the world's highest cable car, but we're only going to use the lower section of it, and we'll hike from the mid way station. The upper part goes to the summit of Mount Bolivar but it isn't functioning. Jefferson tells me that it was built in three years under the last military dictatorship regime, and now a faulty section is taking seven years to be fixed under the democratic government. It was supposed to reopen two months ago, but two men were killed when it was tested, and thirty-seven people had to be evacuated by rope through the floor of the swinging cage. All of this is at 13,000 feet. Jefferson is probably telling me something of his political leanings, but I'm thinking that it might have been built too quickly.

We disembark and eat a couple of sandwiches. Jefferson was named after our second President, and his middle name is Lindbergh because he was born on the anniversary of the transatlantic flight. His parents had hoped to emigrate to the United States, but never did. My guide has a degree in geophysics and his normal work is with oil exploration teams. He volunteers with mountain rescue units on the weekend. We set off at noon.

It's misty so there are no soaring vistas to gladden the heart. In fact, my heart is soon pumping desperately for oxygen, particularly on the uphill stretches. After an hour, it's pouring rain and I'm glad that Jerry persuaded me to wrap my clothes in plastic inside the backpack. But I feel water seeping through my clothes, and my thighs are sore from the previous day's sunburn down at sea level. This is very rough terrain, and we don't pass any dwellings. There are just narrow rocky paths, mile after mile, and my legs give out after four and a half hours.

We make a decision. It's not a matter of choice. If I walk, I'll fall and at this point we're hiking above a long drop. The place we're aiming for is two more hours away at the glacial rate we're progressing. My guide is a tough guy, but he can't carry the bags and me. So, Jefferson will run, yes, run, to Los Nevados. That's our destination village and it's going to be our staging area for climbs during the next three days. Jefferson will rent mules at the village to carry the luggage and me. He leaves me with his big backpack and his camera case.

The only place I can shelter myself is beneath a shallow overhang. It's the base of a tree and the earth under it must have been eroded ages ago in a mudslide. There are gnarly old roots hanging down, dripping water. The ground there is spongy moss. Even scrunched up, I can't completely get away from the constant rain.

Before he sets off, Jefferson explains that I have food, first aid and a flashlight. He says that they're in his pack, with extra batteries. He estimates his running time at about 30 minutes. He's a 28-

year-old marathoner who says he caught mountain goats for his father as a boy. Then it would take him 45 minutes to return with the mules and their drivers. This would bring him back to my inadequate overhang by 6:30pm or at the very latest 7pm. He mentions that daylight, coincidentally, should last until 7pm.

After he's gone I become more aware of my immediate surroundings. I can see where we came from, but the path disappears around rocks so I can't watch how fast Jefferson is moving. Very close by, I notice large ants and I dig in my pack for one of the valuable plastic bags to sit on. Maybe the ants won't chew through it. Incredibly, I decide to read the latest *Granta* for a while. It's great writing and stops me looking at my watch, but water drips onto the pages.

I'm not hungry, but making a sandwich will pass the time and possibly alleviate my brutal headache, which may be caused by the altitude. There's only ham and cheese, which is what we ate at the cable car station, but I dig down in the pack and come up with an apple and a mandarin orange. I try not to look at my watch, but then I worry if it has stopped. It's a waterproof wind-up from L.L.Bean so I want to swivel the knob just in case. This is difficult because the ends of my fingers are numb with cold. I take off my sopping wet gloves and try my spare dry socks. They help, but it is difficult to eat and turn pages. Forget the book, the light is fading anyway.

We've come along a well-used trail that village people use every day. No one has passed me here though, it's probably too late in the day. But what would I do if anyone did come by? What would we discuss, even assuming that someone spoke English or I could remember enough Spanish? Locals would probably speak an Indian dialect anyway. So I might say that I'm waiting for a friend, and if they come across him on the trail, please tell him to hurry.

My watch says 7pm and I frantically search Jefferson's pack for the flashlight. I can't find it but my numb fingertips do locate the extra batteries. Jefferson's pack is sturdier than mine, so the batteries are dry. However, they're not much use to me without the flashlight.

As the vegetation around me becomes less visible I start thinking in the twilight of all the things that could have delayed Jefferson, temporarily or permanently. He fell on the trail, and was lying injured. No one would rent him a mule. The mules and their owners would have hauled their loads early in the day. They would have finished hours ago. Certainly, they would have eaten and settled in for the night. Why would they go out again, in the dark? Maybe they would, but now they're all at the bottom of a ravine. Do mules have night vision? Do their drivers eat carrots? Jefferson had not mentioned money. Who was going to pay, and how much? What was my rescue worth, and to whom?

As usual, I should have asked more questions back in Merida, or even back in the States when I booked the trip. As usual, I should have not overestimated my own physical resources. As usual, et cetera. It's inky black around me now, with the very last trace of daylight rimming the distant mountaintop. I figure that I'm here for the night and my teeth are chattering. Everything on me is thoroughly soaked. My arms are clasped around my knees to keep me from shaking. I'm on a flat surface so there's little chance of falling, but if I move around I could easily end up in the ravine. The two hundred-foot drop is just at the other side of the path that I can't see now.

I'm trying to remember what percentage of your body heat is lost through the head. Is it eight or eighty? I've taken off my sodden wool beret so my only head covering is the nylon hood of my woefully inadequate rain jacket.

Sitting upright on the plastic bag, which has now merged with the muddy moss, I try to settle in for the night. I crouch into a fetal position. An hour or more passes, I think. The only sound around me is the gurgling of water down through the mountain streams into the ravine below.

Then thick rough fur brushes my hand. Christ! What is it? I can smell the animal near me, but is it a wolf or the only South American bear, Orso Andiro? Are there coyotes or mountain lions in Venezuela?

Seconds later, Jefferson appears with a flashlight from around a bend in the path above me. A gaucho leading a horse and a pack mule follows him. Crouched in my shelter I'm inches away from the muzzle of what I now see is his friendly, big old dog!

AN INTRODUCTION TO TRICKLE UP

The Trickle Up Program is an international micro-enterprise program that provides $100 conditional grants to disadvantaged families or small groups of people who want to start and expand their own businesses. Selected beneficiaries agree to invest the seed capital in a business of their choice, work at least 250 hours per person over a three month period, and save or reinvest 20% of their profits back into the business.

The success of Trickle Up is that poor people establish a business using their own creativity, knowledge and ingenuity. The Trickle Up Program has helped people start over 94,000 micro-enterprises in 117 countries since 1979. This activity has affected the lives of 600,000 of the poorest people in the world. 66% of the people they help are women, and almost 50% of the entrepreneurs are under the age of 27.

Trickle Up works through Partner Agencies as coordinators in each region. These are organizations that are already active in grass-roots development working with the very poorest communities of a country. Agencies agree to identify and assist families or groups in forming Trickle Up businesses. These coordinators are reimbursed for a very small portion of the costs they incur to implement the program. Their activities include record keeping, business training, and correspondence with the headquarters in New York. These Agencies are also able to link the poorest members of the community with other local development services such as credit banks, health care and education.

Read these two stories, then go to http://www.trickleup.org

TRICKLE UP GOES TO TONGA

"Well, if you're going to stop off there anyway, why don't you find some coordinators for Trickle Up?" Mrs. Leet, as usual, wasn't missing a beat.

I'd mentioned to her that on my way to New Zealand I was going to visit the island kingdom of Tonga. The Leets, Glen and Millie, are the founders of the Trickle Up Program in New York. The organization gives conditional grants throughout the world to groups of abjectly poor people who want to start businesses.

Trickle Up depends on volunteer coordinators in local communities who identify the groups. The coordinators translate the business plans into English and disburse the $100 checks. Yes, the grants are that small, and they're in two installments. The second $50 is only given after three months of success. But that amount of money goes a long way in the Third World. Miracles have been achieved with the creation of half a million entrepreneurs around the globe.

Mrs. Leet wanted me to find coordinators, and by boasting of my travels I'd let myself be set up. I was happy enough to be set up though, because I'm on the Trickle Up Business Council, responsible for helping the organization in the corporate world. This was a chance to add a needy country to their roster, and to see the entrepreneur creation process for myself.

I had the name of the Peace Corps Director in Nuku'alofa, the capital of Tonga. I'd settled in at the International Dateline Hotel and soon I figured out that I could go to yesterday or tomorrow just by crossing the road back and forth. After I'd done that a few times I called the Director. He invited me for a drink at the Royal Tonga Sports Club which was like many ex-pat clubs in former

British territories. Dark wood paneling throughout and traditional English drinks like Pimms No.1 and shandy. On the walls there were photos of past club presidents and cricket teams.

The Peace Corps man explained that now the Club was open to all races. There were no Tongans in evidence. I could tell because they're very noticeably large. But my host was a Japanese-American who had been interned with his family in Oregon during the war. His comment on this was that he probably became a better student than his non-Asian contemporaries, and that the accommodations were probably more comfortable than that which the draftees experienced.

When we got down to discussing my mission, the Director explained that the Peace Corps couldn't work with Trickle Up officially, because its declared focus at that moment was village education rather than economic development. But he knew everyone in town, including the Japanese Peace Corps staff. Until that moment I didn't know that Japan had a Corps, but I'm not up on the global roster of aid agencies.

The next day he introduced me to an Irish lady who was married to one of the Japanese volunteers. She immediately understood and enthusiastically embraced the Trickle Up process of starting businesses with the poorest of the poor. She agreed to be our coordinator and spend time with me before I flew on to New Zealand.

During the next two days I saw flying foxes and the Royal Family on bicycles outside their Victorian-style Palace. Water holes whistled eerily out by the ocean, and in the jungle I was shown a massive arch made of coral. It was used for worship before the various Bible Fundamentalist groups and Mormons took over the local religious culture. The Peace Corps Director invited me to a local feast at where we ate lu-pulu which was beef marinated in coconut cream on taro leaves. We washed this down with kava, made from the root of the pepper plant.

Groggily, the next day we worked on business plans. The first one was an activity that fitted in well with Tonga's vocational education program. A number of high school seniors were trained every year in auto and motorcycle repair. As the country modernized there was a clear market for such skills. However, the graduating students had no tools of their own. The Trickle Up grant provided the money for them. The budding entrepreneurs had to complete business plans, to demonstrate that they would not lack for customers. Without this 'spark of opportunity', the families would have been in hock to moneylenders for a very long time.

The second set of micro enterprises was made possible by a circumstance that would only happen once in a lifetime. The King of Tonga, Tupou IV was going to celebrate his 70th birthday in July during the following year. The Ministry of Public Works had promised the Royal family that his department would line the streets with mature plantings, but he had no staff to bring this about. The Irish lady and I arranged that a number of entrepreneurial souls would buy the palm tree seedlings with our Trickle Up grants, nurture them, and finally sell them to the Ministry in time for the Royal Parade.

Other plans would be formulated down the road, but now we had one coordinator. I wrote my report for Trickle Up. Then I bought some postage stamps, to support one of the *established* national businesses of Tonga, and I boarded my plane with a clear conscience and pleasant feeling of accomplishment.

SOUTH INDIA STARTUPS

"So, how do you know that they really get the money?" John, my skeptical partner challenged me, sticking his index finger up in the air.

"Well, you have to trust the Leets." I said, "I mean, they don't personally take any pay and the Trickle Up Program certainly runs lean."

I'd met the founders of Trickle Up, Glen and Millie Leet, many times, and I liked their simple concept of helping the poorest of the poor with small 'spark of opportunity' business grants.

"Yeah, yeah. You've told me scads of times that they run this million dollar plus budget with a dedicated underpaid staff of twelve saintly apostles." John put his hands together in mock prayer. "But you don't *really* know when you give them a donation that it actually helps some poor soul somewhere start a business."

John had that final word on the subject, because I didn't *really* know. We didn't talk about it any more until I told him I was going to India.

"India! For three weeks? You mean I've got to run everything here for three weeks by myself."

We're team partners at a stock brokerage company where he'd have plenty of back up. I have my own life agenda. One item on that agenda is my membership in the Business Council of Trickle Up.

"Blame yourself, buddy. You're the guy who made me want to check out these people for real in the field. If you hadn't been so skeptical I might not have planned this crazy trip in the first place."

At the headquarters of Trickle Up in New York I'd copied the list of their Indian coordinators. In the field, the organization operates through a global network of volunteer coordinators. Some coordinators are Peace Corps or UN field officers and others are clergy and local leaders. They identify applicants for business grants in the communities where they work. They also handle the grant money for Trickle Up and distribute it to the entrepreneurs. First on the coordinator list in the Madras area were the Kousalyas. There was no phone number for them on the list.

Mr. Kousalya owns three motorcycle taxis in Chromepet, a village outside Madras, and his wife is a teacher there. They became volunteer coordinators for Trickle Up because they are co-presidents of the Centre for the Development of Disadvantaged People (CDDP). On purpose, I hadn't written to tell them I was coming to India. My wife Rosy thought that was sneaky, but I didn't want them to put on a show.

In the Madras Ashok Hotel Rosy looked at my coordinator list again and reminded me that it didn't show a phone number for the Kousalyas. The hotel manager couldn't find a directory for the area and the phone operator spoke only Tamil. Finally, the Ashok head porter offered to send his cousin thirty miles out to Chromepet on the local bus to deliver a message and get confirmation—that they would receive us. It would take the cousin all day and the charge was less than half the price of breakfast in the hotel.

By dinnertime, he'd returned and I knew that we were expected at the Kousalyas the next day. Another of the head porter's cousins spoke English and had a car. He would take us out to Chromopet and translate for me. I didn't want to depend on any script that the coordinator might have.

That night I rehearsed the questions I would have the driver ask the groups who were supposed to have received the Trickle Up money. John had written them. Over the years that we'd worked together, John had leavened my enthusiasms with caution, and I hoped that I'd remember his advice about making the questions open-ended. Rosy said that she'd remind me and that she'd have some questions of her own.

"You are so welcome, sir and madam. Please enter my house."

Rotund Mr. Kousalya stood aside for us to enter his cement block dwelling and he presided over a little ceremony. He dabbed red powder on our foreheads with his thumb and we were draped with garlands of flowers. I noticed an elaborate pattern of sprinkled sand in front of the doorway. I wanted to ask so many questions about the rituals and caste situation, but Mr. Kousalya deflected me and we went upstairs to his office. The door bore the CDDP acronym and local maps papered the walls inside.

Mr. Kousalya proudly displayed Trickle Up business plans on a table. All his entrepreneurs were illiterate, so he had to put their ideas on paper for them. He explained that the success of a business often meant that for the first time a child in the family might go to school. Education had to be paid for here in India and was a luxury for most of the poor.

The maps on the office wall were for some survey work that he did for the Ministry of Agriculture. Something to do with water pumps, if I remember correctly.

"Can we go and see some actual businesses now?" I said. He agreed that we had two hours before lunch would be prepared.

In Kousalya's area, although the street was not paved, it was swept. I think that it was a relatively high caste district. We squeezed into one of his scooter taxis and drove half a mile to the other end of the village. My driver from Madras came with us and gave me a hard time about leaving his car. But the streets were too narrow for it anyway. I'd agreed to pay him extra for his unbiased translation when we encountered Trickle Up beneficiaries. We swayed through dusty streets, dodging several cows.

At this other end of the village, nothing in the public areas had been swept, and we picked our way through foul-smelling garbage. People here were low caste, what Gandhi called 'harijans' or 'children of God'. Houses here were made of oddments, 'multimedia' items including big, old, weathered billboards for Kingfisher beer. The dwellings made me think back to the homeless in Giuliani's New York and I remembered that Trickle Up had an Initiative planned in the city, for people coming off welfare. Here, in India, there didn't seem to be any social services from which people had to be weaned.

I was introduced to three different families with sewing machines. The ladies were making children's clothes. A wholesaler or someone who owned a factory would pick them up and the clothes would be folded and packaged there. In each place I asked my driver to find out how much money each family had received. They each reported receiving the rupee equivalent of $ 50. When I asked what they had done with the money, they pointed to the sewing machine they had bought second-hand in Madras and showed me the items in their account books. They might be illiterate, but they had no problem with numbers and basic data entry.

In one house, the ladies insisted that my wife sit and work the treadle herself to prove to us that the battered old thing worked. At another house, the matriarch sewed my name and the words Trickle Up on a small cotton square.

On the way back to the Kousalyas house we visited a dark, fetid one-room shack filled with fibrous woven bamboo frames.

The driver announced, "Mushroom growing business."

The frames were constantly watered by the family members who also lived in the room, and mushrooms could be seen on some of them (the frames, that is) in the humid gloom. The Trickle Up grant had been used to purchase spores. The man who rented them the bicycle to get the mushrooms to market had also received a grant to buy spare parts.

This business was at the second and final stage of Trickle Up largesse. It had been in operation for 90 days and the three family members had worked a total of 1000 hours on the project (250 hours more than the specified minimum). Twenty percent of their profit had been ploughed back for more materials, and Mr. Kousalya was about to submit a report to New York detailing this activity. He would then be authorized to pay out their second $50 grant. The mother told my driver that they wanted to buy cardboard boxes so that they could raise their mushroom prices and sell directly to the hotels in the city. They also wanted to buy their own bike because they thought that the rental guy was ripping them off.

Simple business stuff. But to me it sounded like vertical integration straight out of a B-School syllabus. Following the Trickle Up process, after that second grant they'd be on their own and Trickle Up would survey their progress from time to time.

As we came back into Kousalya's house I could smell curry and lunch was ready. The building was two rooms up and two down. I'd already visited the office upstairs and assumed that a bedroom was also up there to get night breezes. The rear half of the downstairs was the kitchen with a privy in the yard, and the front room was used for everything else. The cement walls were painted bilious green and there was a long narrow window along the top of one of them. A naked, low watt light bulb hung from the ceiling. A TV in the corner was draped with a crocheted altar cloth and in the center of the room there was an unpainted concrete platform. It was our table.

The ladies of the household ate in the kitchen and my driver ate in his car. Maybe they all had eating utensils. Mr. Kousalya and my wife and I out in the front room certainly didn't have any knives or forks. I'd read enough about Indian customs to know which hand to not use for eating but I was glad that nothing required cutting and that it was vegetarian fare. Finger-lickin' good without the dead bird.

Children had been peeking through the plastic strips covering the doorway watching us eat, but they stood back at the end of the meal when two ladies came in. They were carrying a sitar and another stringed instrument made from a gourd. The sari-clad ladies were introduced to us as colleagues of Mrs. Kousalya from the local school. They played gracefully and at length.

After their recital I was astounded to be asked to perform in some musical way. So I gulped, coughed and sang an old British Army marching dirge "Lloyd George knows my father, father knows Lloyd George . . . " Designed for long marches, it repeats itself endlessly but without the variations of Indian music. I tried not to look at my wife as I sang.

Inside and outside the house spirited applause followed. The entertainment over, Mr. Kousalya belched, smiled and heaved himself to his feet as he heard a car pull up outside.

"My brother-in-law. He will now take over the transportation."

This meant that Ravi, the brother-in-law, would take us all to another village to see a business project and then he would drive us back to the hotel in Madras. So I sent our hired car and driver back to the city. Thus, I'd lost my independent translator, but at this stage I certainly felt satisfied about the honesty of the Trickle Up process. In the village we were going to, they wanted to show us mature businesses that had been thriving for a couple of years or more.

Mrs. Kousalya's brother Ravi provided a conversational change of pace. After the car had been blessed and garlands strewn over its hood, we set off. Ravi was an actor temporarily at liberty. He explained that he introduced the local textile tycoon to hot young starlets, and thus he had the occasional use of the company car. His chunky frame and patrician good looks had earned him steady work in the local Tamil film industry. On the way out to the village he would turn his head grinning. He wanted to make sure that we folks squashed in the back got the punch lines of his film biz sagas. Mrs. Kousalya sitting up front with him nodded to us in support, so nobody was watching the road. After we hit a couple of axle wrenching potholes and a herd of goats, Ravi concentrated on the rutted track and eventually we came into the settlement.

There were about fifteen thatched mud huts, pigs, chickens and some of the scruffiest, skinniest people I'd ever seen. I didn't have to ask anyone where these people fit on the social ladder. They were tribal. This meant that they were even below the level of the Untouchables we'd met at the unclean end of Chromopet. This kind of settlement could only exist a safe distance from the communities of farmers in the area because, according to Hindu belief, the use of village facilities by the tribals would pollute the water supply on which life depended. Riveting Ravi had commanded our attention on the drive here, so the Kousalyas had not had the chance to tell us about the settlement. It was a total shock.

Many of the people had rushed out of their huts on our arrival and they crowded around us, chattering. The body odor was overwhelmingly pungent to me, but my after-shave might have nauseated them too. Many men were brandishing what turned out to be the item they'd each bought with the Trickle Up grant money. It was a bellows. The last time I'd seen this kind of bellows was when my father kept bees in England. He'd sedated them by putting damp burning paper into the bellows and then pumping smoke into their hives.

Well, they didn't have bees here, but the business of most people was catching rats for the local farmers. Unchecked, the rats would eat the precious grain. The tribal families were paid to coax the vermin out of their holes and clobber them. Until Trickle Up came along with the money for the bellows they had scared the rats out with their lungs. They'd lie on the ground by the entrance to the rat holes puffing away with smoking rags.

Several men demonstrated for us. They mimed themselves coughing and pointed to the rows of dead rats hanging on a string near the huts. The men put two fingers up as they pointed to the rats, and grimaced at their own inefficiency. Then they squeezed the bellows. With the aid of these magnificent hi-tech tools they indicated there was no coughing and the smoke was more focused. With all the fingers of both hands outstretched, they happily assured us that their rat harvest was now plentiful and that they were on the road to riches.

Hey, John, I thought, you really should get out of Wall Street and see this. Trickle Up works in wondrous ways, my friend.

My wife's whisper brought me back to South India.

"Don't ask what they do with the dead rats."

We shook hands with all the rat catchers (to their great surprise) and we set off back to Madras. My wife and I were too stunned by what we'd seen to say anything further and even Ravi was mercifully silent. At the hotel we assured the Kousalyas that we would give a full report of their activities to Trickle Up. This I did when I got back to New York.

In the office John was suitably chastened when he heard my tales and saw the photos. He even pulled out his checkbook and made a significant donation. Wonders never cease.

Now it's two years later, and although the business projects uncovered by the Kousalyas are doing well, Trickle Up has to move on and cannot give them any more grant money to distribute. The Kousalyas have done nothing wrong, but with a limited budget and the need to practice what might be called grant triage, Trickle Up has decided that some provinces in Northern India are more in need of their help. They really mean it when they say that they help only the poorest of the poor.

The Kousalyas have torridly expressed their dismay at this situation to me in letters galore. You could say that these dedicated coordinators are victims of their own success, but in Trickle Up's world there just aren't enough 'spark of opportunity' grants to go round.

MY INDUSTRIAL-STRENGTH SUMMER

It was a prospecting trip. I worked for an investment bank that prided itself on its global reach. In 1997, the firm was just starting to look for megadeals to finance in the newly independent countries of the former Soviet Union. It wasn't in my job description to go to the region, but I knew that the team responsible for that activity was seriously overworked. I figured that if I were able to show them some viable projects, I'd be up for substantial finder's fees.

Our minimum sized deal is $20 million. Why the minimum? It costs the same for accounting and legal legwork whatever the size of the deal. But underwriting fees are always a percentage, sometimes up to 5%. So, the bigger the better. I'd set myself a daunting task, however. There was no proper commercial law code in Ukraine, land was still owned by the state, and government permission was still necessary for almost everything.

The idea that I might actually find something viable was bolstered by my friendship with Sergei, the only Ukrainian I knew. I'd met him in New York when he was depositing some of his own finder's fees in our bank. Before the Communist demise he'd run the largest computer factory in Eastern Europe, supplying all the Soviet Union. That job had given him contacts in every ministry and hundreds of factories throughout the empire. Sergei now had loan brokering agreements with a large number of the managers of these organizations. Many of them had gained ownership during the chaotic privatization drive. They needed every adventurous Western financing contact they could get. My banking company was well known, and my business card said Vice President. Unbeknownst to them, I was one of hundreds of VPs.

Apart from the monetary motive, I was intensely curious about a country seven years in transition. Ukraine is the size of France, and it's populated by 53 million souls. I had no knowledge of the language, and I created a laminated 3x5-file card in my shirt pocket just to be able to read the Cryllic alphabet. At my New York office I had to explain repeatedly to fellow workers that it was not Russia, and the only comment was: "Strange choice for a vacation, Ukraine." Even Sergei's wife Anastasia said it when I arrived there. Family and friends knew of my delusions of grandeur and itchy feet. They just sighed and didn't offer to join me.

Day One... "Did you notice the Russian toilets?"

Sergei was leading me out to the Kiev airport parking lot. I'd had to use the toilet before we left the terminal building. Okay, yes, they were the step-and-squat variety, but he was making the point that they were a Soviet legacy that he deplored and derided.

I commiserated and he then pointed out 'his car'. It was the largest Opel model, with a driver standing by. I was duly impressed but it turned out to be owned by a friend who'd been dragooned for the day. Sergei's own car, a Volvo, had been stolen. Unfortunately, this had happened just as he was diligently considering the features of competing auto insurance plans before paying his premium. It was my first example of Sergei's preference for details over decisions.

We had a nice ride along leafy boulevards past classy looking condos into Kiev and the Hotel Dnipro.

"In ten minutes will be here the guide female, for your city touring."

Sergei had faxed me that he had set up a 'saturated' program, so I should have expected no allowance for my jet lag. Actually, in retrospect, I was most grateful for the three-hour personal tour with a professional. It gave me a sense of the city's dimensions and character so that I could explore later on my own with at least a rudimentary perspective. The guide spoke excellent English and this alone made me want to thank Sergei for his thoughtfulness. The highlight of the tour was visiting St. Sophia Cathedral with its domes upon domes and breathtaking icons.

Then Sergei let me settle in. My room at the Dnipro was furnished in birchwood with orange Formica trim. Electric outlets were in unexpected places on the walls. It was as if groupings of furniture had not been placed according to the original plan for the room. I napped for a couple of hours before meeting Sergei later at the hotel restaurant. We had vareniki, which is Ukrainian ravioli, for dinner. The plan was that we were going to be in Kiev four days, then travel south to Odessa for a while, and return back to Kiev. Some meetings were arranged and others were hoped for.

During the meal I noticed for the first time that Sergei had an outrageously long nail on the little finger of his right hand.

We were expected at the Ministry of Aviation the next morning.

Day Two . . . One of the basic problems about high level lending to Ukraine, I'd been told, was that Ministry of Finance permission was needed to pledge any assets as collateral for loans. This permission was essential, as it would also carry the central government's guarantees of repayment that Western banks required. But the impression of most people that I spoke to was that the International Monetary Fund did not want the national assets pledged. In fact, the IMF would withhold aid if the guarantees were given. It was a financial Catch 22.

The Minister of Aviation had heard of leases. He indicated that he thought that, as a financing tool, they might be a way around the permission block. I had to explain how they functioned. In later meetings with Ukrainian CEOs and ministry officials I brought up leasing whenever I could. I hadn't a clue whether this financing structure would pass the IMF ban, but it seemed to give these beleaguered executives hope.

The Minister had a production line of Antonov jets, the flying workhorses of Central Asia. The production line was halted though because the new prospective buyers needed financing. The Minister wanted to tap the non-military market, so he needed some retooling money for the Antonovs. I think it was to be used for sealing up the aircraft gunports.

The Minister was a bristly haired man with good posture. He gave the impression that he would be more comfortable in a uniform. No doubt he had been raised and trained to regard Western capitalists as his archenemies. He seemed uncomfortable having to share his needs with me. I tried to imagine a Pentagon official dealing with someone on the opposite side of the Cold War if the US had gone through the changes Ukraine had experienced.

We ate cabbage soup and dark bread in the Ministry cafeteria.

That afternoon Josip flew in from Moscow. He's Georgian and he exudes energy. I know him through another connection and now we met for a brainstorming session in the suite he'd taken at the Dnipro Hotel. It was time for me to change gears and hats. So far on this trip I'd been Sergei's loan angel-person. Now I would be Josip's access to Visa Gold debit cards.

Josip had an intriguing idea. He was putting together a VIP club package for the Soviet nouveau super-riche. "These are people who will pay $13,000 a year to be permitted entry to a special lounge at Moscow Airport," he laughed. "And they will still pay $30 every time they use it!"

Josip's package for a modest $5,500 annual fee included a live mobile phone, discounts at top hotels, gifts from Cartier and an umbrella with a wooden handle. Among other things, members would also receive a Visa Gold card with miles and gift points. This was where I entered the picture. As it would be a debit card, the members had to deposit at least $2,000 each in our bank. As he planned to sell one thousand memberships in six months, it looked like a good income flow for our bank. My bonus would blossom and some of the members might become substantial investment accounts.

Josip's background is journalism and his English is flawless.

After the period of perestroika he somehow owned a printing plant. His fortune was made rapidly when he obtained rights for Western glossy adult magazines. These had never been available in Russia and Josip experienced the joy of seeing lines of provincial Russians queuing up at his kiosks in Moscow. These buyers were taking the girlie magazines out to the culture-starved hinterland for resale.

Josip and I worked on some details of his VIP club plan, then we went to dinner with Sergei. It was fascinating for me to watch these two guys, disparate in so many ways, but with the same language. Josip, the wild man with homes in three climate zones and a Midas touch. Sergei, the nerd with quirks and political clout. I didn't have to worry. Like people the world over they found their common ground and created rapport. In their case it was based on business. Josip suggested that Sergei should publish an article about creating business plans, and Sergei described to Josip some favorable clauses in the new securities laws of both Ukraine and Russia.

"So what's the best club, Sergei?" At 10pm, I was yawning but Josip obviously felt that the night was still young.

This part of the conversation was in English and I could tell that Sergei was mentally processing the word 'club'. Was this 'club' the safety device that he should have put on his Volvo, or was Josip asking about the VIP situation in Kiev?

"Club, Josip? What kind of club?" Sergei looked anxious.

"The best, my friend, the best in Kiev! We have to show our guest here that business is not so boring . . . like in New York!"

"Ahh, nightclub you mean." Sergei was catching on. "Only my daughter goes to such place, but I will ask here the waiter."

We were directed to the Hollywood. It was in a cavernous former bus garage and the walls, floor and ceiling were painted in black and silver stripes. By this time, Josip's cousin Merab had joined us. He was in town from the Georgian Republic to collect a debt. He was huge, his torso a perfect cube. The four of us were the only customers in the Hollywood.

But we were not alone under the flashing lights, shouting to each other in Georgian, Russian and English over the heavy metal sounds reverberating through the old garage. The dance floor was full of women.

Very soon after we arrived, a flock of them waltzed in formation around our table. They waved and smiled, then all except one they went back to dance. The remaining woman, older than the others, pulled up a chair next to Josip and they spoke together in Russian. Lap dances were arranged for all (surprise, surprise), and they were performed with grace and vigor. Or was it vigor and grace? Whatever, it stopped my yawning.

In the cab ride back to the hotel, Sergei told me some of the things that had been discussed in Russian at the nightclub. The Georgians had described me as an important Western banker who'd arrived from America in his own jet, and that big Merab was my bodyguard. We'd left the two Georgians at the Hollywood. Maybe they would make a better deal for the services available because of their important American connection.

Day Three... There were two meetings that next day. The first was with the man whose team writes the business plans for Sergei. These are the first step in his investment banking work. He won't agree to search for money unless the entity develops a business plan with him. The team does market research, cost analyses and profit projections for companies in any industry in Ukraine. A very efficient set up and it was a surprise after the lack of sophistication at the Aviation Ministry.

Our contact in the afternoon was with a 'fixer'. Vladimir Lubachenko was someone who supposedly could guarantee that the President of Ukraine would lend his support to any project Vladimir showed him. We were to be allowed to bid on three of the deals, a chemical storage facility, a textile factory and computerization of the customs department. Vladimir chain smoked throughout the meeting and his teenaged daughter translated for us.

A fast forward . . . We won't ever find out whether he can get those guarantees because three weeks after I left the city Vladimir dropped dead from a heart attack. So the three projects are on hold, but Sergei now writes to me 'he hopes for reanimation'.

For two whole weeks I lived with Sergei's fractured English and his palpable anxiety with completely understanding me. Back home I reflected on the fact that I'd never spent so much time with one person translating everything for me. But at least then we'd had the instant back and forth of correction and explanation while we were together.

Now his e-mail and faxes to me are written on his computer with the aid of something called Stylus. It's an instant translation program that frequently gives me a chuckle or a puzzle. Sergei applies a scanner to my replies then he puts them through Stylus. So I constantly have to try to anticipate what figures of speech Stylus will garble in Russian. Yes, Ukrainian is a separate language, but Sergei is an ethnic Russian like many of his countrymen.

Back to Day Three . . . That evening we had dinner at Sergei's apartment with his wife Anastasia and Ruslan, their twenty three-year-old daughter. Ruslan is a medical student and she sells Mary Kay beauty products in the hospital where her mother is Director of Obstetrics. Ruslan has never heard of the pink Cadillac recognition program. Here, the Mary Kay top award is a silver Mercedes.

As mother and daughter were leaving for vacation together the next day, providing dinner for a business guest must have been a major imposition. But if there were irritations among the family members they didn't show. The space in which the three of them live is miniscule, and this is classed as a luxury flat. It was one of the first condos in the city and it's situated in an area of foreign embassies.

We spent a delightful evening with much joshing of Sergei

about his late night. He had given them a sanitized account of the Hollywood visit. The culinary piece de resistance this evening was some fish liver. I was to remember this delicacy vividly, on a succession of toilets during the days to come.

Fortunately there were no meetings scheduled for tomorrow. I'd have a day to myself before we would take the night train to Odessa.

Day Four . . . I loped around the city sightseeing. In the meat market a woman crossed herself when I took her picture. She was standing next to a mountain of sausages.

I'd taken my French anti-diarrhea pills first thing that morning but they didn't seem to be as reliable as on other trips when I'd experienced gastric disturbance. I checked out of the overpriced Dnipro and, as arranged, took my luggage to Sergei's for storage. He said that I wouldn't need a jacket and only one tie for the three days in Odessa, and I was going to be staying in Ruslan's room at his apartment when we came back.

When Sergei told his wife, the doctor, about my physical condition she insisted on plying me with some soft black pills. They tasted of chalk and the black coating was hard to wash off my hands. Sergei had his own favorite remedy for diarrhea, and he took a large quantity of pink capsules for me with him to the train. Medically, I'm pathetically trusting.

Before we left I was included in a nice ritual. Ukrainian families have a tradition at family farewells. They sit in silence for a few minutes looking intensely at each other and on this occasion I was family.

Sergei had booked us a sleeper compartment and the berths were very comfortable. We had sandwiches packed by Anastasia with us, and the attendant brought glasses of tea on a lace cloth. Sergei insisted that I take the lower berth. Smart move, because in spite of the medley of medications, I made several trips during the night to the bathroom at the end of the corridor. The decor there was riveted aluminum with scarred black slimy plastic fixtures. Because I was going out into a public area I had to get half-dressed in the dark each time.

The number of stops the train made further complicated my situation. We halted at every station during the three hundred and fifty miles. The attendant diligently locked the toilets for a sanitary zone before and after each one. In spite of the nice tea she'd brought us, I could have killed her.

After twelve hours the night train to Odessa pulled into the magnificent station there. As we walked down the platform Sergei pointed to the number on the side of our train. "Here is the reason why it takes so long. Under Soviet rule, all trains were numbered in sequence of importance. Kiev to Moscow is still the Number 1." Our Kiev/Odessa train was number 55.

Day Five... Anatoly met us at the train that morning. He's the CEO of an engineering works employing 3500 people. He's also the founder of the Rotary Club of Odessa. We piled into his Volvo and sped off into the countryside. Wearing seatbelts is mandatory in Ukraine, but no self-respecting male will do anything in compliance other than pull the belt across his chest. And this is only done with a laugh when approaching an intersection where police might be hiding. The officers love to catch someone unbelted, it's a perfect bribe opportunity. Once we were out of the city, Anatoly and Sergei in the front seats ignored the bright red flashing seatbelt light on the dashboard of the Volvo all the way for an hour to our destination.

This turned out to be the holiday camp for Anatoly's factory workers. Small one-bedroom huts were set in the woods, back from cliffs overlooking the Black Sea. Every family had a dog. The cabins were equipped with simple kitchens but they had no running water. The one and only bank of toilets were 'Russian style' and they were outside the communal hall. Here, squatting amid clouds of flies and mosquitoes I experienced that defining question so many travelers ask themselves. "Why? Oh, why am I here?" It's a feature of all the difficult trips that I later remember fondly.

As the sea was adjacent to the camp, we had a refreshing swim, but it was very windy. Sergei finally wore the Yankees cap I'd brought him from New York. The cap enabled Sergei to deal with the wind. It protected his hair, which was always plastered in greasy strands across his broad bald head. I hadn't seen him do it, but he possibly uses that fingernail to comb the strands.

That evening we had a sumptuous dinner at Anatoly's hut with his extended family. Other guests included the local congressmen of the ruling party. Our host was a leading fundraiser for them. There was a very attentive silence when one of the politicians reported on his visit with the President of Ukraine up in Kiev a few days before. This was the inside track, I was later assured. Internal factory policies and business activities would be adjusted accordingly.

By now I'd finished my French pills, Anastasia's soft black ones and a handful of Sergei's pink capsules. When my physical condition was described to our dinner host as my excuse for eating lightly, yet another remedy was suggested.

"More vodka! It's the best cure in the world!" Well, it made me forget momentarily, and I still don't know which remedy or combination was finally effective.

That night, before we went back to the city of Odessa, I learned the traditional sequence of toasts. Honored guests, family present, absent friends, world peace, universal prosperity, etc. To each one I silently countered, "Stable stomach!"

Our home for the next few days was a ten story workers holiday hostel, on the seashore side of Odessa itself. It was owned by another factory whose CEO we were scheduled to meet. The hostel was not fit for anyone but workers who could afford absolutely nothing else. It was free for us too!

Day Six ... The water and electricity had been turned off throughout the hostel building during the night. Doors banged, floors and beds creaked. In the morning the shower was cold. I gave the floor lady a couple of CDs and an elaborate cosmetic kit so that she'd do my laundry. I didn't envy her the task, but from the sounds I'd heard from the rooms on opposite sides of mine I guessed she'd experienced worse clean up jobs.

We went to Anatoly's office after breakfast. He was ready with his presentation and factory tour. The plan for the company was conversion from military electronics to consumer goods. In an unused facility he also wanted to start producing ethylene oxide—for antifreeze, among other things. There is no Ukrainian producer of this basic raw material and he figured that his output would also be competitive enough to export.

Lunch and all our succeeding meals in Odessa were at an elegant private restaurant. It had been owned by the Communist Party and now was used by whatever party was the leader in the endless coalitions. Anatoly's party had their turn this year.

The food was substantial, but it was the same at each meal. Each event started with caviar, plates of ham, bologna, and salami, with stuffed eggs and sour cream on the side. Pork or veal chops followed, along with the rest of the sturgeon's body. The vegetables were always fried cauliflower, tomatoes, onions and peas. Melon and vanilla ice cream for dessert. Jugs of thick fruit compote, mainly apricot, were always at hand. With lunch, champagne, cognac and vodka were optional, but at dinner they were de rigueur to fuel the toasts.

After the first of these meals, Anatoly had one of his staff walk Sergei and me around the central part of the city to see the sights. We needed the exercise.

Odessa was never bombed during WWII so the center looks pleasantly homogeneous. The Soviet style monstrosities are on the outskirts. Chestnut tree plantings over a hundred years ago make it as leafy as Kiev, but there's a close, cozier feeling in Odessa because the streets are relatively narrow, though not medieval alleys. The main growth of this city was from the 1700s through the 1920s. At the turn of the century the population was one third Jewish and to me all the people there looked less Slav than in the north. It's five hours from here by ferry across the Black Sea to Istanbul.

Our afternoon meeting was with the Governor of the province. He had his own interpreter and an economic aide in the meeting. Although he asked me if I knew Pataki, our New York State Governor, he was basically unfriendly. I got the impression that it was only Anatoly's clout that got this meeting set up, and this pompous ass had had to be brought in kicking and screaming. To boot, the economic aide was sarcastic—and they wanted to borrow half a billion dollars from our bank for general administration of the region. I don't anticipate a realistic business plan from these guys.

Day Seven... The factory that morning was called Uranus. Anatoly's establishment the day before was called Mercury. Venus tomorrow?

At the office complex, we first visited with the chief engineer. Over the engineer's desk there was a large, classic picture of a studious Lenin, and the engineer noticed me staring at it.

"We haven't bothered to take it down. It was our lives for a long time. He wasn't Stalin or Beria, you know."

The engineer then explained how they made compressors, and before I fell asleep with boredom we went into the CEO's office. I didn't ask him about the identical Lenin portrait over his desk. After a chat about his ambitions for the company we set off on a tour of the gloomy echoing plant. As had happened at Mercury the day before, our visit coincided with the workers' lunch break.

"May I take photos?" I said bravely. "They'll be sort of... before..." implying that there might be an "... after," with our infusion of cash.

The boss looked startled at my request, but he nodded and I pointed my camera at the only person near a bench. The machine operator was slightly built, and dressed in gray overalls. He had thick filthy glasses on the end of his gigantic nose. A troll I thought, or maybe a gnome. Whatever he was, he grinned at the attention and the CEO then muttered what I imagine were the Russian words for, "Do some work!" The troll didn't exactly become a blur of activity, but he bent over his machinery, thus spoiling my shot.

After this we went to another area where we were shown the world's ugliest automobile air conditioner. This was their post-Soviet new and improved state-of-the-art consumer product. It looked powerful and crash proof. I'd vomit if I ever had to look at it inserted into the dashboard of any car I might own.

Today, there was a working lunch. We met Captain Selchuk, another friend of Anatoly. The Captain had been allowed to buy 100 of the 6000 ships of the national Black Sea fleet. Only 2 of his 100 freighters were operable. He had no money to use them though. He'd come up with part of a solution and wanted to present it for my financial consideration. The scrap value of the other 98 ships would give him working capital. Brilliant, but the nearest cheap breaker's yards were in India and Captain Selchuk couldn't even get the 98 rusting hulks out of port. I listened, looked serious and ate enthusiastically.

"After lunch, we meet one of my friends, just a guy from our school time together." As he said this, Anatoly winked at me. It was an inside joke that I didn't get, even when we pulled up at City Hall.

It turned out that Anatoly was boasting about his connection with the Mayor of Odessa whom I found to be an impressive figure oozing charisma. As in some other parts of the world, the Mayor was very much as odds with the Governor of the province in which his city was located. There was a noticeable contrast in their styles too.

A group of well-informed and likeable trade aides properly supported the Mayor. We chatted about the Internet and how to structure municipal bond offerings. These loans are well favored by bankers because of the security of the tax rolls and the collateral of the city's infrastructure. In theory, if the city doesn't pay the bank, we might seize the sanitation trucks or something.

Mayor Hurvitz asked after Rudy Giuliani whom he'd met twice, that was twice more than my score. Then he presented me with a glossy illustrated tome about the city and a diamond-studded medallion. A world class guy, I thought. Let's lend him some dough!

As we walked back out into his anteroom there was a flash of lights and a microphone was pushed into my face. I deflected to my Ukrainian spokesman and Sergei was grilled on what we had talked about with the Mayor. That night our images appeared on national TV and Sergei assured me, oddly without prompting, that he hadn't promised my firm's money to anyone.

On we went to the offices of a Lebanese banker. His investment need was for a department store that the bank had repossessed. It was three quarters finished and had a great location between the railway station and the biggest outdoor market in the city.

That evening I was guest speaker at the weekly meeting of the Rotary Club of Odessa. Hey, it was Tuesday. Remember that song? '...And the Rotary meets on a Tuesday night!' I gave my stump speech about the various forms of corporate financing. By now, Sergei also knew it by heart, but he still paused as if he were translating it live. During the chat after the speech, I met some bulky street traders and another shipper with scrap metal problems. I imagined the port of Odessa clogged with hulks.

A boozier dinner than usual was consumed that night. The shipping guy joined us, as well as the visiting Madam President of the Rotary in a city called Sumi. The jokes flew thick and heavy. Lots of hearty male stuff for her benefit, with one about the silent stone lions outside the library in her city. Everyone has heard this old standard with the punch line: "They only roar when virgins go by." I guess it's a joke that is applied to any municipality that has statues of lions and women.

Day Eight . . . Before breakfast, I packed for the evening train back to Kiev. The night before, there had been so much partying on the floor above me that the gaudy chandelier had fallen down and I had to step around glass shards that were embedded in the swirly-patterned green carpet.

That morning we met the President of Odessa Telecom. As in other countries phones are still part of the Postal Service so the boss man had the grandest office in a grand old building. But the whole city and surrounding area is woefully short of voice and data lines. In Odessa, unless you're a well-connected business man, you must visit this grand building just to phone the next town, never mind the next continent. Five hundred million dollars was what the Prez had in mind. I agreed that it would be a project big enough to at least gain the attention of our bank and that there might be some equipment companies who would come in on the deal.

After lunch, Anatoly tried to get us into the Opera House which was being restored. But even his clout wasn't enough to convince the construction foreman. That was a pity because after looking at the photos in the Mayor's book, I guessed that the Jewish cultural establishment of the city had outdone the opera house builders of Budapest, Vienna and all points west.

That evening we enjoyed a farewell banquet. It was the same menu, but with toasts to everything and everyone. On the train the bunk beds didn't seem so bumpy, but maybe it was the massive infusion of vodka my body had received during the evening.

The train chugged northward, back to Kiev.

Day Nine... A creepy guy who had sat in on our meeting at the Air Ministry the previous week was waiting for Sergei and me at the train. He was wearing the same acid purple suit that I'd inwardly winced at the week before. Also, his hair still looked as if it had been dyed with shoe polish.

He'd heard that I'd expressed an interest in art and as we rode in the taxi towards Sergei's flat the guy assured me that he would personally escort me to galleries owned by his friends. I agreed that the discount he would negotiate for me was extremely tempting but I begged off. My excuse was that Sergei had arranged so many meetings for me that these visits might not be possible. I suppose that this was some sort of test I was giving to Sergei. He proved to be a true friend and confirmed to the creep that I'd be too busy. The art procurer asked to be let out at the next intersection.

"No sale, smarmy pants," I muttered, then I thanked Sergei for his support.

"Is normal." He shrugged. "Is normal for him, is normal for me."

I let it go at that and felt cheap. By now I had a clear sense of Sergei's honesty and fairness. His self-serving activities were natural and he was always completely open about every person's interest in a deal.

When we arrived at the flat he retrieved Igor the cat from his neighbor. Then Igor had to be fed and fussed over. There was much intimate sounding baby talk in Russian with such cooing and stroking, that I felt like an intruder. Maybe Sergei's long fingernail was really for tickling the cat. I hadn't had the nerve to ask any of the humans and Igor only miaowed in Russian.

Sergei demonstrated the pullout bed in Ruslan's room complaining that it was made in East Germany and that, against his best judgement, his family had pestered him to buy it.

We made the following deal with each other. We agreed that Sergei would make breakfast, lunch was up to each of us to find and that I'd take us both out for dinner each night. Sergei now needed time to draft and mail the fee agreements while our encounters were still fresh in everyone's mind. He also wanted to remind all our prospects to work on those essential business plans.

I went for a walk in the city. Glorious weather. I found the restored old Golden Gate to the city and a faded hotel called the Grand Ukraina. It had been the Party hangout—dated elegance, departed power. On the way back I passed through more markets. The traders seemed gentler here than I remembered in Russia, and another contrast was that in my two weeks in Ukraine I saw no public drunkenness.

Back at the flat Sergei wanted to show me his home office/hi-tech environment. The workstation seemed to be able to do so much that I was surprised it hadn't made breakfast for us. With all its elements it took up half the tiny living room and seeing my friend in his swivel chair I imagined him as a one-man band with fourteen instruments attached to his body parts.

We ate at Miami Blues. Standard American fare but sour cream with everything, and prices much higher than at Wolfies on Collins Avenue. But at Wolfies in Florida there are no Ukrainian starlet-bimbettes with lupine eyes to distract a man.

When we got home I went to bed early with a serious headache and a case of the sniffles.

Day Ten . . . Woke up feverish with the flu, sick as a dog. Lumpy though it was, Ruslan's pullout bed was a refuge, a nest and most welcome. I was through the fever by nightfall so I got up for dinner and we ate at Layally.

It was Lebanese and the ubiquitous sour cream fitted right in. The portions at Layally were very large and neither of us felt like finishing them. I tried to explain 'doggie bags' to Sergei. He was still processing my morning announcement about being as 'sick as a dog' so this took quite a while. He said he could never ask for a bag in a public place, but then we both burst out laughing as a waiter took two plastic containers to a nearby table. 'Take-out' translates pretty easily.

Day Eleven . . . This was our day for Lavra. Absolutely not to be missed, it's a monastery and Orthodox Church complex that has been in existence since before the first millennium.

High above the Dnieper River there are golden domes in profusion. There's green trim on a dozen snow-white basilicas. Most of this historic area was missed during the wartime bombing, but there are a couple of ruins to remind one. Underneath it all is a labyrinth of caves and tunnels where monks have always lived and died for centuries. To go into the tunnels you buy a dripping wax taper with an inadequate paper hand cover. The passageways are just wide enough for one person. They're whitewashed, silent and cool. Bearded robed monks sit praying in alcoves down there and, every so often, around a curve you smell the tallow mixed with incense and you encounter a dead monk laid out in his wall slot. Just writing this makes me want to go back in there to experience the spooky sensual atmosphere again.

Even though the tourist trivia questions bubbled up in my mind I didn't really want to know all the scientific stuff about constant temperature in the tunnels. Also I thought I'd rather not learn about the social lives or personal hygiene of the monks. Sergei didn't foist any such knowledge on me. His socialist and scientific background has left him cynical about religion. I'd asked him if he ever went to church.

"No," he said, "is for Anastasia. She is traditional . . . but is not for me or my Ruslan." He smiled proudly.

After lunch he went back home to his loan agreements and I explored the monastery gold museum. Afterwards it was a splendid long walk back to Sergei's, then on to dinner at Miami Blues.

"She is wearing good Italian shampoo. The other one, the blonde, she is wearing Mary Kay, the cheaper floral, I think." Sergei was nodding to himself as he told me this.

We were bimbette-watching at the restaurant, and two spectacular ones had swayed close to our table. I laughed at what he'd said, thinking, this guy is lightening up. But no, it was with this serious declaration that Sergei revealed his self-styled extraordinary sense of smell.

I expressed amazement at this skill and he played it down saying that the attribute was a burden. He claimed that the sense was so strong he could also diagnose women's ailments, particularly backaches. The gift ran in the family. His mother and her mother had been able to do this, he said. As his wife and daughter didn't come back home from vacation before I left, I wasn't able to get any corroboration. Asking the two passing bimbettes in Ukrainian? Forget it.

Sergei had enjoyed my amazement that evening, so he performed for me frequently after that. Apart from the gift itself I was impressed by his familiarity with the brands of fragrances. Since I've been back in New York I've thought about recommending him to friends at Avon. They're just breaking into Ukraine and they'd pay well for consultants. Their questions might be:

"Hey, guys, let me know. Can he do it? Is his hooter that hot? Is his proboscis that perceptive?"

Day Twelve . . . This was a Sunday and the Computer Market was open. We had to go, for software and CDs at counterfeit prices. In the subway on the way out to the Market we passed a kiosk selling all the latest movies on tape for $3.99.

In the afternoon I continued my shopping in the streets of the Podol district. I'd had requests from friends for Soviet military headgear and hip flasks. The equipment for sale in Podol is new and plentiful. I reckon that, even though troop levels have been drastically reduced, the factories are still turning out the same stuff as before. But now it's for the tourist trade.

Back to the apartment and Sergei who had produced more agreements for me to check. He'd only had a few signed before I'd arrived in Ukraine, but my performances were calculated to persuade the reluctant. I was amazed that Sergei was able to obtain exclusive money raising contracts with these firms. In other words, he would be paid his fee even if the client company found money by their own efforts during the contract time.

"They need me," he shrugged. "They have already asked everywhere."

That's encouraging, I thought cynically, but he told me that in four years of activity he had found twelve chunks of money. I was impressed, even without knowing the size of the deals or the percentage of his fee. His money was salted away somewhere and later that evening he showed me a video of the $750,000 apartment he wanted to buy north of Miami.

We ate at Cantina Mexicana, and after tasting the food I'm sure that the chef did not speak Spanish. Curry powder in the gazpacho?

Day Thirteen . . . I treated myself to a country excursion. A car with driver took me ten miles out of Kiev to Pirohovo, a 300-acre pastoral theme park. There were just a few visitors and no rides. This was a government project (weren't they all?) to show the architectural and life styles of villages from all around Ukraine. There was a great variety of thatch patterns, window sizes, fireplace shapes. It covered a number of square miles, with long walks between the villages.

Resting on a bench against a stone wall I was regaled by a tourist from Hamburg. For him the Ukrainians could get nothing right. His best travel experience ever, had been a ride on the Concorde. I told him that my personal best was right now, doing whatever I'm doing. He couldn't relate to that and he stomped off with his group.

I loaded up with hand painted eggs at the quaint gift shop. Couldn't stop myself buying as many as I could safely pack, they were so vivid. A book that I bought with them described the ancient timeless meanings of the symbols, like the spirals for fertility. The shop owners gave me an out of date promotional calendar. It did more justice to the village scenes than my camera would. Since I've returned home I've sent them a calendar of American small towns. I hope, though, that they put it up at home rather than in the shop.

Our guest at dinner that night was important. Katya is a GYN patient of Sergei's wife Anastasia. Katya is also the Finance Ministry official in charge of relations with outside bodies like the IMF and the World Bank. A heavy woman in her fifties who chain-smoked, she gave us an update on the guarantee problem that we'd encountered at every loan meeting. The problem, she explained, was internal not external, but that didn't make it sound easier to solve. It probably just meant that bribery and corruption was even more important than I'd already figured it to be.

This meal was at Uncle Sam's. It offered good quality coffee shop fare at Beverly Hills prices. But it's where the local elite wants to go. And if I do score with any of these deals, Katya can certainly ease the process.

This was the only place where I saw bodyguards. They all had shaven heads, no necks, double breasted suits over black t-shirts, and shiny, square-toed shoes. They ate at appropriately located tables. Far enough away for the boss to have privacy with his bimbette, but near enough to act quickly if he were threatened. There were three sets of these characters at Uncle Sam's that night, with matching chauffeurs and wheels outside.

Day Fourteen, the last day... There was one more meeting before we went to the airport. Sergei's contact was a developer from Dniepropetrovsk. He'd made the six-hour journey to meet me. I was conscious of how awkward his blueprints must have been to carry. He spread them all out on Sergei's coffee table.

The living room had been rearranged for this meeting because neither Sergei nor the developer wanted to spend money for a hotel conference room. The project involved shops, offices and apartments. It sounded viable and I learned that his city might be larger than Odessa. Also, I learned that over the course of the century it had supplied more leaders of the Soviet Union than any other.

I promised that during my next visit...

I'd finally run out of steam. Had this all been a colossal waste of my time? That was something to consider of course, but now I needed a vacation.

THAI TALE

He walked beside me along the street, negotiating the crowds, chattering about his life. He was hard to ignore.

"I am Paul. Paul, that's my *Western* name. I want to practice mine English."

At first I was rude, untrusting and irritated. My megadeal had fallen through, and I couldn't get a flight out of Bangkok till the next day. Then he started talking about his work and I found myself listening intently.

He sold insurance to the new Thai middle class and I warmed to him, sharing his frustrations. By then, we were walking in unison, matching feet forward, dodging the vendors and stepping over the steaming puddles left by the monsoon rain.

"So hot!" I wiped my forehead with my shirtsleeve, "It's so humid, your country." Paul was wearing a suit and tie but it didn't seem to make him sweat. He nodded.

"May I invite you for a river ride?" He smiled at me. "It's cooler out on the water." I immediately thought a little less of him because I now cynically assumed that his 'cousin' owned a boat conveniently nearby.

"It's quite exciting." He giggled. "They have car engines and go very fast."

I'd been thinking about doing the ride that day anyway, but not with a bunch of blue-haired American tourists. Although travelling solo brought you more in contact with the country, there was no one to share the 'Oohs' and 'Aahs'.

So far, Paul hadn't touted a family boat connection. He was pleasant company and a free guide, so I said "Great, let's do it."

We turned off the busy street and walked down a block to

where houseboats were lined up along the riverbank. Gangplanks connected them to each other. I followed Paul, wrinkling my nose at the sewery water below. Some of the houseboats had the long prowed snake boats tied alongside and Paul said something to each of the boatmen. I guessed he was angling for good price for us. Then we stopped on the back deck of a houseboat and a woman brought me a cold Coke while Paul chatted with a stone faced wrestler type who was wiping down his snake boat engine. The boatman reminded me of the chunky Asian character in one of the James Bond movies.

Paul told me how much to pay 'Oddjob' and I gave him the money. It seemed a bit high so I assumed that I was also paying for Paul's ride. So, he wasn't a free guide, but so what, it was fair enough.

We set off at high revs. The water churned behind us like some sort of high pressure chocolate vat.

Paul pointed out the Royal Barges in their gilded boathouse. We passed by the five star hotels. I couldn't see mine, it was a few blocks inland. I was sitting up front. Paul behind me was talking into my ear over the roar of the old Ford engine. Occasionally I looked back past him and Oddjob's muscular forearm was rippling as he held the long tiller steady.

After about fifteen minutes on the river we headed into a congested area. It was chock-a-block with houseboats and the motor gurgled in protest as we made our way through. Paul hadn't said anything for a couple of minutes. I wondered what we were supposed to see in this mess and I turned around. He wasn't in the boat. Then I saw him nimbly stepping from one houseboat to another. He was about three boats away from us. I stood up and yelled out his name. He turned, paused just a second. He waved and disappeared into a houseboat. If I'd been nearer I'm sure I would have heard the giggle.

Suddenly I fell back in the boat as Oddjob found a gap in the river traffic and opened the throttle. In no time we were out in mid river and there were no landmarks that I recognized. There were ratty little shacks on one side and a swamp on the other. Oddjob slowed down and headed into an opening between stands of bullrushes. I couldn't see anything over them and sweat was running down into my eyes anyway. Then he cut the motor.

I speak no Thai, but I recognized the rubbing of thumb and forefinger together. Carelessly optimistic I shook my head, and then wished I hadn't. Even though Oddjob didn't need a weapon I gasped when he reached into a pocket. Talking rapidly in Thai he pulled out a scrap of paper and a ballpoint. He wrote a number on the paper and tapped it with his huge fist. It was the same number of baht that I'd given Paul. I raised my eyebrows, pointed to the number and did a 'from me to you' gesture. This earned me a big nod from Oddjob. I moved to his end of the boat and peeled off the money. Immediately he whipped the tiller around and fired up the engine. With a grin he shook my hand.

Done deal. Not a megadeal, but a deal nevertheless.

KIWI KINDNESS

I fell off the motorbike. Actually, it was a motor scooter, the kind that true bikers scorn. The model that I'd rented was a Honda 250 Elite. It had a comfy seat, adequate power, and an upright driving position that made it great for touring and sightseeing.

But scooters have small wheels, with donut tires. What you gain in comfort, you might lose in traction. And when I came over the crest of a hill along the remote East Cape coastline of New Zealand, I hit gravel. I hit it the wrong way and skidded. The view out to sea was spectacular, and because I could see the view so well in that upright position, I hadn't noticed the road surface.

When I heaved myself up from the ground, I was shuddering. Every part of my body seemed to be throbbing independently. A flap of flesh was hanging off my left hand, and the raw pulpy bleeding stuff was full of gravel. My left arm and leg were badly scratched, and my clothes were torn, but my hand was the worst part. It made me want to throw up to look at it. If it hadn't hurt so much, I wouldn't have believed that it belonged to me.

The bike had gashes in the paint along one side, clear through to the metal. When I stood the machine up, the steering column was out of kilter. If this couldn't be fixed, I'd be riding in circles for the rest of the trip. The light switch mechanism at one end of the handlebars was mashed. I would be riding circles in the dark. My bag containing a month's vacation gear was scuffed up, but serviceable. A couple of the bungee hooks holding it on the bike had separated.

This examination process had taken some time, and I think that maybe one car had passed. I'd been too shaken to notice. As I'd skidded ten feet in from the edge of the road, the people in the car hadn't noticed my condition. In fact, if I'd skidded another ten feet, I would have sailed right over the cliff.

I knew from looking at the map that morning that I was now only a couple of miles from a village called Tarukau. The name made me think of the Pacific Islands that I'd stopped at on the way to New Zealand. Now I was starting the last week of my vacation, circling the North Island.

I tried to take the bike with me down to the village. This did not work. Even holding on to the handle bars as if I were making a U-turn, I could not make the bike move straight forward. So I set off on foot and left my gear on the disabled bike.

Having no choice, I hoped that anyone who was coming along the road to or from the village would take pity on me. Of course, someone could steal the bike if he were going south, as I was. But then I'd see my bike in the back of a dusty pickup and lay myself on the road. Or, if someone were heading north towards the bike, maybe the driver could be persuaded to turn around for me.

God only knows how I was lucid enough to figure all that out. If only I could think out business decisions so well, in an uninjured state. Anyway, I know that I couldn't have carried anything with me, because I needed to hold one hand with the other. The flap of flesh seemed important.

Tarukau was an intersection of roads, not much more. I saw a gas station, post office, and a general store. They stood across from a grand war memorial with a patch of grass in front and a border of white stones around it. There was a crowd of people around the front of the store, and I got some stares as I went in. Later on, it was explained to me that Friday was check delivery day, and that every government benefit dollar from pensions to Maori tribal support programs arrived on that day.

A stocky light haired man behind the counter looked at the blood on me and said, "You look like you could use a cup of tea, mate. I'm just brewing a fresh pot."

"That would help," I answered, "but first, though, do you have some antiseptic cream and a bandage?"

He pointed them out on the shelves back in the store. Then he told me I could use the employees' washroom in the rear.

"As soon as I take care of this lot," he motioned to the crowd, "I'll come back there and see how you're getting on," he said," and your tea should be ready by then."

I pried the gravel out with my fingers as best I could. Then I used the sink, running cold water on my hand until it stopped flowing pink. Then I wrapped the bandage around my left hand. I'm left-handed, so securing it wasn't very easy.

There was a knock at the bathroom door, and the store guy said, "Your tea's up, come and sit outside." I came out and he introduced himself as Steve Locksley. He looked at my bandaging effort, and pronounced it good enough for the next half hour. He declared that the pace would be hellish until he closed at noon. It was Saturday and these people didn't want to wait through the weekend to spend their money.

"When I've locked up, I'll look at your hand, then we'll go back up the hill with my truck and see if we can do something about your bike."

Outside the store there were a couple of benches, and I sat and sipped the tea. A valuable vestige of Empire, this tea. Steve Locksley was serving a strong cheap Indian blend. As if to the manner born, he added heaps of sugar, and a touch of milk. I told him that it "hit the spot"—something no one would say here in New Zealand, or even in the mother country. Even though I grew up in England, to everybody here I was definitely a Yank.

While I was waiting for Steve, a young woman pulled up in front of the store. She was riding a real bike. Her's was a 750cc Norton, a real growler. She was kitted out in studded black leather, with a World War I German officer's helmet on her head. When she climbed off the bike, she pulled off the helmet by grasping the spike on top. Then she shook her black hair out, and stretched herself like a cat waking up. She ordered a cold lemonade from Steve through the service window on the front wall of the store, then she sat down with it next to me on the bench.

"Look like you bin in the wars then, mate." She nodded at my hand and ripped up clothes. I explained about the gravel, and she promptly expressed the opinion that scooters were "bleedin' death traps." I nodded and bitterly agreed with her.

At some point earlier in this trip, I'd spent a somber evening in the company of a vacationing Scottish neurologist. At home in a teaching hospital he worked on spinal injuries. He was traveling by car and he warned me that I was taking my life in my hands. He'd explained his theory that the greater the cc rating of a motorbike, the more likely the chance there was of serious injury. I remember that in the nanoseconds after crashing his theory came into my mind, and I'd actually drawn some comfort from the thought that my Honda Elite wasn't so powerful—but I didn't get into this with the lady biker.

She was telling me that in her opinion the Norton 750 was the best machine on the road, and she also mentioned that this particular one did not belong to her. Her name was Leslie and she was an Aussie.

"Just over here in NZ getting away from some horrible bloke, this silly bugger who wants me to have babies with him."

She told me that she was looking after a herd of cows further down the Cape, for a friend who had a farm. He'd gone away for a month leaving her in charge of the place. She'd found that the cows could mostly fend for themselves, so she was exploring the area.

"It's handy that his girlfriend is my size, and that his head's no bigger than mine." she said, twirling herself around, "and of course, he doesn't know that I'm on his bike. But, no worries, Craig. 'Cause I used to work sheep for my father with a bike."

By this time Steve was ready. I introduced them to each other and Steve became a livelier person. He made a suggestion that included both of us.

"Hey, look. We're going to head up to my house and fix up Craig's scooter." This was the first I'd heard of it, but it sounded good to me. "First though, we're going to cool off and go swimming." That sounded whacky, but I was hot and I was in his hands. For the moment I wanted to ignore the rest of my physical condition.

I looked at Leslie. She shrugged and said, "Sounds good. I'll follow you on the bike."

First, we went north up the hill and loaded my stuff into the truck. Then we came back through Tarukau and drove about three miles south and stopped at a river. There was a bend in it near a bridge and a pool had formed. It looked cool and deep. Nothing was said about swimwear. The three of us just stood there looking at the water, then Steve and I followed Leslie's lead as she stripped. The two of us achieved immediate male bonding, grinning at each other as she shed bra and panties and jumped in.

"Ooh, it's cold. But it's ggggreat. Come on in!"

I just waded in. The cold water was bracing and I tried to keep my hand dry. Steve elegantly dived off the road bridge and surfaced near Leslie. She splashed him vigorously every time he came near her.

After we'd become thoroughly cold, Steve climbed out of the water and handed us blankets from inside the truck. They were itchy and furry.

"They're for my dogs," he said. Leslie commented that she liked the feeling of being wrapped in an animal skin. Then we drove a few miles further south and turned into his driveway where five German Shepherds formed a welcoming party.

Steve's place was partially finished, but comfortable enough. The living room had a huge stone fireplace. In the kitchen there was a large TV which was tuned to CNN whenever he was in the house. The house was unfinished because Steve's ex-wife still held part ownership. He said that they had some unresolved issues. There was only one bedroom on the ground floor, but he showed us the bare upper floor which was littered with plaid sleeping bags.

"I get visitors, sometimes a lot. Take your pick." We'd talked about what he needed to do to the bike, and he'd looked at my hand. He put some pungent salve on it, telling me that it worked well for the guard dogs, but I would need to stay a couple of days so that I could heal. In the meantime, he would fix the bike and Leslie offered to help him. I didn't know whether they'd turn out to be Dr. Mengele and his biker babe assistant, but for the moment I felt nurtured.

There were two small fields between Steve's house and the road. In one he kept a few steers and in the other field he was growing corn. From the front verandah there was a great view of the ocean less than a mile away. Behind the house the land rose steeply to a barbed wire fence. There was a gate in the fence and an outdoor toilet next to it. Beyond the fence Steve grew half an acre of marijuana.

We had a delightful two days. Now most of it is a blur, but I healed well! Maoris dropped in at all hours for a chat and some non-traditional exchange of gifts. We ate fish that we caught off the rocks at the edge of the Pacific, and one night Steve made a fragrant beef stew. He introduced me to everyone as his Wall Street friend. He showed the visitors my business card with a wink, as if he had millions stashed with me. He frequently chatted up Leslie, but she joshed him and kept her distance.

On the bright sunny morning of the third day, the bike was aiming straight again and my hand was good enough to grip the controls. I'd already seen most of the highlights of North Island so I was going to skip Wellington and circle back up to Auckland for the flight home. Leslie pocketed my business card and said that she ought to get back to the herd at her friend's farm.

The three of us said our good-byes, promising to write. I told Steve that I couldn't thank him enough for his kindness, and he promised to think of some ways that I could. Leslie rode along with me south for a mile or two before she revved the Norton and growled off into the distance.

We did stay in touch though. Steve sent me a letter, mostly about dogs. A friend wanted to buy the German Shepherds to guard his farm and Steve thought that he would replace them with Rottweilers. He asked me to get him some information from the American Kennel Club on the breed, and I wrote back for clarification on some point. I also asked if he'd heard from Leslie because I hadn't. She hadn't given us an address, as she wasn't sure where in the world she was going.

Steve didn't reply for a year, and then he had a sad tale to tell. His ex-wife had "shopped me to the narcs." They'd burned his back field and taken his dogs. He'd done some time, but he said that it hadn't been too bad as he'd been assigned cooking duty because of his store experience. But before he'd been nabbed he'd salted enough away to pay off his wife. So now the house was his, and he was definitely planning on owning a patrol of Rottweilers. I sent him the Kennel Club information and promptly received a thank-you note with a photo. Steve now had a Maori girlfriend living in, and he hadn't heard from Leslie.

But *I* did, a few months later. One morning the fax machine by my desk in New York rolled out a short letter from a motorcycle dealer in Sydney. Leslie had just started work in the office there. It was her first clerical job. She wrote that I was the only person she knew who had a fax number. It was a surprise to hear from her, as this was almost three years after my trip.

She also mentioned that she was pregnant, so I guessed that the bloke wasn't so horrible after all. I hate cute endings, but if it were a boy, maybe they'd call him Norton, after the bike.

FOOT BY FOOT ACROSS ENGLAND

Ever since I read that someone had mapped out a walk across northern England using ancient footpaths, I'd been itching to do it.

I grew up on the northern side of the Trent River. It's part of a cultural dividing line between the sophisticated, but shallow, South, and the gritty, vibrant Beatle-producing North. At the age of 24 I moved across a much wider body of water to settle in New York City. Most of my visits to the UK in the intervening thirty-plus years had been to London and areas south of the Trent.

Now, there was the physical challenge of fifteen straight days of hiking. It would require about eight hours of walking a day. People call it the Coast-to-Coast. Detailed maps are readily available, even in New York. The web of pathways stretches over 200 miles. Apart from the physical challenge, I anticipated a massive blast of glorious nostalgia.

My wife Rosy expressed interest in the project. She has borne my expatriate patter for so long that she smells of Imperial Leather soap and eats Marmite on toast. However, she doesn't like flying. So she blocks out all thought of the journey until it actually happens. She packed a variety of footwear items, and a collapsible chair. She's an American and supremely self-confident. Also, she's always claiming to be fitter than I am, so the idea of the strenuous hike didn't faze her.

It didn't faze me either. I walk through Central Park to get to work every morning. That's at least a half hour, five days a week. I felt that by crossing that mass of urban granite and foliage daily, I was more than ready. It wasn't until I got hold of the British

Ordnance Survey Maps, with their tightly drawn gradients and icons labeled bog and crag that I started to focus on what I'd determined to do.

Group travel hasn't appealed to me since I was a tour leader during college when I had to deal with coach-borne tourists. Their cliques and group dynamic became more important than the sights they were seeing. Walking now with differently paced hikers en masse would be an unacceptable irritant. However, there are clear advantages to having one's heavy bags carried by someone else, and to knowing that there is an arranged and paid-for bed at the end of a tiring day.

A dilemma, to group or not to group. Then I'd read about the Coast-to-Coast Packhorse service, which not only shuttles luggage [and blistered humans] by van, but also arranges bed and breakfast bookings within striking distance of the paths at strategic daily distances. I was sold. We'd use Packhorse and go by ourselves. We didn't need a group.

"Done deal, Packhorse people. The return to my roots, English masochism at its best. Two trekkers heading west to east, starting May 30." Now pounds sterling have been duly prepaid so we can't back out. No second thoughts. This is it.

Arrival at St. Bees . . . If you look at a map of the British Isles, you'll find the coastline of Cumbria and the town of St. Bees just below the Scottish border on the left. We were going to start from that coast and head east. This meant that we would cross three distinct geographic regions. First, the Lake District with its gorgeous mountains and deep narrow bodies of water. It has inspired poets for centuries. Next, we'd pass through the Dales, the seriously cute part of Northern England, almost in the same way the Cotswolds are for the South. Finally, there would be the Moors (think Heathcliff). They're mostly unpopulated with scrubby vegetation. Even the ubiquitous sheep prefer the lusher western areas.

We arrive at this western headland by train from Manchester and we're booked into the Queens Hotel up the High Street from the railway station. We have separate rooms. This is bliss for the first night because Rosy cannot accuse me of snoring and depriving her of sleep. She's jet lagged and she crashes in her own quiet room. I'm raring to go, to try out my new boots, check out the terrain, and enjoy the parade of senses that being back in Northern England is bringing on.

At 3pm I walk over the grassy fields through a couple of four-house villages. In England, any settlement of more than one house has a name. Virtually every building in existence is on an ordnance survey map. In order to make a loop I approach St. Bees Head at the north end and walk it against the wind. The Coast-to-Coast Walk does the opposite, but I'll be doing that with Rosy tomorrow. The English teacher from the local boarding school whom I'd met in the pub when we checked in reckoned about 2 hours maximum to get round the headland. He said he sees between 20 and 40 walkers a day from May to October, but only about 20, all told, during the winter.

Fierce wind, sheep-cropped grass and I'd forgotten how many wild flowers grow in these parts. My mother had been a primary school teacher in the Midlands and she'd taught me the names of every one. There are cowslips and bluebells around me, and the bright yellow gorse on prickly bushes. Sea birds nest or rest in the hollows. Up on the headland it's colder than I expect and the extra woolen socks I dig out of my backpack make useful gloves. The hike is also taking longer than I'd thought, even though I'm moving quickly to keep warm.

Back to the Queens Hotel at 6:30pm and Rosy is still dead to the world. By the way, that English teacher probably hasn't hiked the headland in 20 years. During those years he's probably unconsciously shortened the estimated walk time when he meets new inquiring visitors.

I feel physically efficient; weary but ready. At least the boots will be fine. There's a saggy bed, and I nap for a few minutes. I wake Rosy at 7pm for dinner. There's excellent pub food with splendid Cumberland sausage. I try three different pints of bitter and sleep like a log. In the morning I'm surprised to be roused by traffic, forgetting how busy these little villages are early in the morning. I'm glad Rosy's room is at the back of the building.

Day One—St. Bees to Cleator-14 miles . . . We start off about 9am with bracing high winds and the sea churning froth. I resist a mild temptation to dip my toes in the ocean, or to pick up a stone to carry it eastward. I leave no note in a bottle nor any inscription in the sand. We'll know what we've achieved when we finally get to the East Coast.

A mantra comes to me as the two of us walk along the headland. It's circus music, the kind they play when the clowns come out: *"Tah-rah-rah, boom dee-ay."* With lots of brass and a drum that you hit on both sides.

The wind is less fierce when we move off the headland around noon. We descend into a village and decide to favor The Dog and Partridge with our lunch business. Along with a couple of foaming pints, the barman offers tuna.

"Brown or white?" he asks.

Rosy says, "Brown. It's coarser, but better."

"I'll stay with white," I tell him. "The brown sounds like cat food."

The barman looks perplexed and pained. It turns out that the choice of brown or white is only for the type of sandwich bread not the tuna.

Rosy changes her footwear in the pub. She says that her feet feel liberated in the Teva sandals. The paths after lunch are mainly farm lanes and fields. We meet a few cows that don't say a word to us, and we note the various styles of stiles set in the hedges and fences. They let people through, but not large animals. There are V-shaped versions that would challenge even the slimmest person wearing a backpack.

A serious hiker passes us. He grunts "Eric, Coast-to-Coast," and gives us a little salute. He's properly equipped with a plastic map bag hanging round his neck. His face wind-burned, he strides ahead of us, calves bulging. We decide that he's harmless, but probably a fitness fascist.

I mean, don't get me wrong, we're serious too. That is, our quest or mission is serious, but we feel a ridiculous and misplaced satisfaction in attempting fifteen days of hiking without much preparation and fancy equipment.

Through the village of Cleator, Rosy develops a stitch in her thigh, and after another half mile to Black Howe farm, it's obvious she can't go on. There are no public phones on these paths and the farm ladies don't offer use of theirs (they're probably fed up with hikers and their problems). So I walk on a mile or two to Cleator to get transport, leaving Rosy settled but frustrated on her folding stool.

I finally get to Ennerdale Hotel and the assistant manager agrees to go off and pick Rosy up using the hotel car, it's a Bentley. He buys eggs for the hotel at Black Howe farm so he knows the place well. This is a world class hotel, an old mansion, quite an upgrade from the Queens pub the previous night in St. Bees. Our luggage is there, courtesy of Packhorse. There are elegant gardens to stroll in, but first a glorious blissful toe-wriggling bath. The room is done in knotty pine. It's the latest decor fashion in England, and a relief from the high gloss enamel traditionally used on indoor surfaces. I'm luxuriating in the bathroom for quite a while before Rosy arrives. The hotel car ran out of gas, so the driver had to walk back to the hotel and get another car, his own Mini.

The Ennerdale serves us a stylish dinner, big choice, good food. There are no other Coast-to-Coast hikers in this hotel. So, other than the Eric the Red this afternoon, we've met no other hikers.

Day Two—Ennerdale to Rossthwaite-14 miles . . . It's a lovely sunny morning. Rosy is going to travel in the Packhorse van with the luggage today to rest her balky thigh. A pretty waitress from the hotel gives me a ride to the trail. She's from a local farm family. Her grandpa still goes up on the hills in February to bring down the sheep. He does it with dogs. They're black and white border collies. I've seen them in every farmyard. Grandpa owns 3100 sheep and 300 cows. The waitress granddaughter wants to go to America and I readily offer my help in New York.

The path is rocky, with some moderate climbs along Ennerdale Water. On the map the lakeside walk looks easy, but where the mountain falls straight down into the deep water you have to climb up and over each promontory. I believe that it has been proven that humans can imitate sheep if the humans are avid enough hikers.

Drizzle starts. Today's mantra is *"Incy wincy spider..."* I press on to the woods at the end of the lake before stopping to chew on some raisins. But there isn't much cover, and anyway water drips on me from the trees. It's time to break out the heavy duty yellow poncho. Although there's no one to share it with, I regard this as an exciting moment because now I feel justified in having carried it around. Actually, walking inside the poncho is OK. Now there's no wind and a good flat path through a pine plantation.

The first person I meet today is carrying a sheep skull. He's approaching from the east and it's hard to know what to say to him. I could try: "Hey, where'd you get that?" But it's pretty obvious where he got it, with sheep all over the place, eating, shitting, and breeding. Quite frankly, I'm amazed that I haven't already tripped over a bone or two myself.

After deciding against a Yorick joke, I settle for: "Looks like it might dry up nicely." I let him figure out whether I am referring to the weather or the skull.

Then three cyclists careen past me. I'd not thought of this as a bike path. The way forward has now turned into a very rough trail, and I can't imagine riding it even on a mountain bike. When I catch up with them fixing a flat, they tell me that they plan to go all the way to the East Coast. Looks like they'll have lots of portages and time-outs for repairs.

The Black Sail Hut appears in the mist. This is the tiniest youth hostel in Britain. It is the only dry place where I might sit down that I've come across in four hours, and the door is locked. There's a stone bench outside though. I can rest even if I can't get dry. A couple of local people who are walking their dogs come down the path and they tell me that the hostel manager doesn't let anyone in until 6pm.

From this point the path is being "restored" for a mile or two. In the pouring rain volunteers from hiking clubs and environmental groups are moving flat rocks around so that the vegetation won't be trodden down. I stop for a few minutes and give them my blessing. The poncho has made me feel somewhat ecclesiastical. I tell them that the Goddess of Walkers is satisfied with their work, and that soon She will be smiling instead of weeping on them. As if at my command, the clouds part, the sun comes out, and there's a wonderful rainbow.

A few miles on, I find a miniscule pub-cum-teashop at the village of Seatoller and there I enjoy some bonding with other Coast-to-Coast walkers. They are some of those 20-40 walkers per day that we haven't yet seen. They ask many questions about New York City. They can't believe what they've heard about our crime numbers going down. The conversation seems surreal because I can't imagine that anyone in the US would know about the crime statistics of London or Manchester. But these guys all know the details of the latest Guiliani/Bratton fracas for control of the NYC Police Department. Then one hiker tells me he won't visit the USA until we lift sanctions against Cuba. He's been to that island and has fallen in love with someone. "With Fidel?" I ask, and think about beating a hasty retreat.

I take the wrong turn out of a field after leaving the pub. Because of this, I end up doing three extra miles of damage to my feet before coming into the back end of Rossthwaite village. There are so many of these ancient footpaths and bridleways and I'm badly out of practice in map reading. God forbid I should have a neck-slung waterproof map case so that I might look at it more frequently. The lesson learned today is that I will stuff the folded map in my waistband so that I don't keep taking off the backpack to find it.

Mrs. Dunkerley's Guest House is the last building in the village. It would have been the first for me if I hadn't gotten lost and come in at the other end of the only street. Rosy arrived midday but she hasn't yet met Mrs. Dunkerley. The door had been left open with a note for guests to make themselves comfortable. They're trusting souls up here in the Lake District. It turns out that Mrs. D. bakes pies for a local restaurant, supervises a caravan campground and runs her own bed and breakfast.

We have a good dinner in the nearby hamlet of Stonethwaite at the Langstrath Arms, but as it's Saturday night, there is a bit of a wait. We meet an Australian couple, a big bluff white-haired man and his worn-looking wife. They're retired civil servants, from a rural area of Queensland, doing Europe. They have their travel plans mapped out for years to come. I think about my cousin Bill, terminally ill at age 61, and wonder whether he'll get anything of a retirement life.

The tiny cubicle shower in our accommodation irritates Rosy. My own problem with it is not its size, but the complicated instructions on the plumbing and the electrical connections. We've noticed that B&B owners like to pin up their own explanations of the manufacturer's instructions.

Day Three—Rossthwaite to Grasmere-8 miles . . . Rosy sensibly picks her walking days by weather and terrain. If both considerations are not favorable, she rides from bed to bed in the Packhorse van with the luggage. Today looks good for walking. By the way, English people rarely use the verb "to hike." One could muse on the reasons, but "hiking" sounds more strenuous to me so it asserts itself in my mind.

We're getting used to the Northern cheeriness at breakfast and in the pubs at night. There's a lot of self-deprecating humor and teasing. It's like the atmosphere in some rural coffee shops in the USA, where locals hang out and create instant rapport with visitors.

This is a glorious day; blue sky, not too hot. Today, Rosy and I take things very leisurely. It's our shortest day. There's variety in the terrain and excuses to dawdle. As it's the weekend there are hikers, runners, and dog walkers galore. In deference to the holy day my mantra is a hymn, *"All things bright and beautiful, all creatures great and small..."*

Even the climbing part is easy today because of strategically placed large stones. There's a very developed system of trail maintenance here because the Lake District is so popular. The local clubs have been out early today flagging a number of trail changes to let the vegetation recover from the pounding boots. We climb over Greenup Edge, crossing the path that goes along the ridge. There are many of these high ridge paths. Some of them were actually paved and used by the Romans.

It's a delightful sunny stroll down towards Grasmere. There are bubbling streams and Rosy falls in one. Not to worry, she's happy to cool off. We pass beautiful gurgling waterfalls, and when we get to Easedale, there's an ice cream shop that we *don't* pass without stopping! Coming down into the town there are lovely gardens, meticulously groomed.

Our bed in Grasmere is at Mrs. Nelson's Undercragg House in a grand Victorian vicarage. She has good taste in furnishings and it's a comfortable place. We stroll the elegant little town. Considering what a tourist destination it is, the center is barely commercial, with very controlled signage. We ask about the possibility of Indian cuisine in the town but Mrs. Nelson equates Indian food with take-out and says, "There's only the pizza place, but you could try the Carvery. Some Indians own it, I think. Or at least they're foreign." We eat there, but there isn't much evidence of foreign influence in the boiled vegetables and overcooked beef.

Day Four—Grasmere to Patterdale-10 miles... The sun isn't shining so Rosy takes public buses instead of the Packhorse van. The bus goes through Keswick and Penrith so she can explore the towns.

The clouds are dark but I experience no rain until I've been walking a mile or so. By the top of the mountain-of-the-day I am soaked up to the knees and the yellow poncho is billowing around me. By the way, this poncho has been a familiar item in my other (New York) life, as I own a car there that leaks. For years, whenever I've parked the car I've carefully draped the driver's bucket seat with the poncho to deflect the drips. Unfortunately here on the high windy trails the poncho does not drape well and rain gets in around the hood. I'll have to find something to tie it around me.

After another couple of miles the water has seeped through my underwear but, "Lo and Behold," I come across a hut. Through the window I can see a man, but when I yell, he says through the door that he feels bad about it but he can't let me dry off inside. He says that there can be as many as a hundred hikers a day coming through at this time of year.

"Once I let them come in out of the rain, I can't get rid of them." He's opened the door a crack and I can smell some high altitude Columbian brewing behind him. Tabloid headlines flash through my sodden mind: "Coffee-Crazed Killer Hacks up Humble Hermit".

I squish on, my thighs chafing.

Soon I notice that there's white stuff covering my boots and I wonder what I've trodden in. Then I realize that I'm creating foam. It appears every time I take a step, so I slow down and watch it form around my feet as I walk. Finally, I understand that residue soap from my socks is interacting with the hot moisture in my boots. Whenever I move it just keeps bubbling up through the canvas tops of my boots. Awesome!

Even though I reflect at length on this phenomenon, discomfort from the driving rain precludes the mental processes that might lead to invention of a new consumer product. Even though I've probably wasted the moment, I'll never forget it. However, only a very lucrative licensing agreement would persuade me to recreate it.

"*Oh, the navy gets the gravy, but the army gets the beans, beans, beans . . .*" This was the marching song when I was in the Sherwood Foresters Regiment.

There's bad news when I get directions in Patterdale. Greenbanks Farm where we're staying the night is another couple of miles. At this stage, even though the village has all the amenities I've dreamt of for hours, I don't bother stopping anywhere to dry off. It would take too long and I just want to get all my wet clothes off. The material of my trouser legs has chafed my thighs, and my crotch is severely sore. These last two miles are very painful.

At the farm Mrs. Iredale knows walkers and she has a wicker hamper by the door. "Get down to your skivvies, luv. I'll take everything to the drying room, then I'll put the kettle on for your tea."

Thank God for her, and the deep long bath and extra strength lotion.

Three hours later when Rosy arrives (she's walked two miles from the bus stop) her slacks are so glossy wet that Mrs. Iredale thinks that she's wearing oilskins.

In the parlor we meet Eric the Red. He's also staying the night, but he doesn't recognize us from that first day. I'd also seen him at the back of the room at the pub back in Seatoller, but he'd been focused on his maps. He's doing the Coast-to-Coast in eight days instead of fifteen, and he frets if he deviates a yard from the Wainwright Walk Book. Mr. Wainwright spent most of his life researching the public paths and did not speak to his wife for twenty years.

Eric has memorized Wainwright's route, but still carries laminated sections of the map hung around his neck. I envy his waterproof gear which he deprecates as "not the best, but as good as I could afford." I recognize the English false pride of poverty because I've been known to blather it myself occasionally.

He's come twice as far as I have today, in the same weather. Other than sweat marks, his clothes are dry. What an insufferable fellow.

It's a simple dinner here. There's no menu choice, but the food is hearty and welcome. Mrs. Iredale is a motor-mouth, but she's thoughtful enough to have put newspaper in my boots to soak up the moisture. I love her.

Day Five—Patterdale to Bampton Grange-14 miles . . . Rosy is sleeping in, and this is a morning when my ambition to walk instead of ride is sorely tried. It's drizzling and I glumly take Mrs. Iredale's directions, to avoid backtracking those two miles into Patterdale village. I'll pick up the official route highlighted on my map somewhere up in the mountains that loom over the valley.

From the village of Hartsop I take a trail into one of two adjacent valleys. I see a climbing figure in the mist ahead of me so I follow him along a path up into the drizzle. I'm feeling well-prepared for wind and rain today because I have a silken rope from Rosy's commodious survival kit knotted around the poncho.

I'm singing *"Sergeant Pepper, Sergeant Pepper . . ."* It isn't quite a mantra but the Liverpool Lads are with me all the way up, and I recall the time that I tried to sell them four Volkswagen Beetles. (That vignette is the *Yankee Initiative* story. As yet, it is unpublished.)

Getting up to a high ridge in thick fog, I'm really tired after only an hour and a half. The map gives me the impression that I'm at the highest point of the day and that I'll now be making a gentle stroll down to a lake. The sky clears for about five seconds each minute, and during those seconds I have to get my bearings.

I'm at a T-junction of paths, with nothing heading forward and down to a lake. The only boot imprints lead off sharply left or right. Clouds close in but I can hear voices in the mist. Suddenly four stocky Asian men in matching red tracksuits march across from the left in front of me. When I wave my map and ask for help they mutter something in a foreign tongue and disappear to the right up a steep incline. I blithely assume that they're some kind of apparition that hikers experience under intolerable stress at high altitudes.

The wind picks up and I can't open the map without losing it. More voices, they're English this time, and six walkers with a guide appear. For all its remoteness this is a popular area. They tell me I am at least two miles out of my way.

The fog clears briefly and shows the lake below. I stubbornly express an interest in descending (anything to get below the cold windy wet cloud line) but the group's guide assures me that (a) there is no path down, and that (b) if I insist on *sliding* down I'll plunge into Windermere (five miles off my route). I'd come up the wrong valley and I'm looking down at the wrong lake. I need to see big signs, like the one over the hills in Hollywood. There's no choice but to go with the group. It's almost a vertical path up slate scree and my worst climb ever. I have to make equal use of hands and feet, and I can only see one person above and one behind me.

We make a lunch stop. It's out of the gale force winds behind the wall of a sheep shelter. The Asian quartet is already there, squatting on their heels, scooping up their rice with their right hands. They nod to me in unison. The guide tells me that he's come across these men before in the Lake District. They're Ghurkha mercenaries from Nepal, training with the British Army.

After lunch we hike along the Roman road aptly called High Street, and at this point we're so far up that I'm the nearest to God that I'll ever be on this walk. There's a long high ridge called Kidsty Pike and then a gentle gradient down through a pine forest down to the correct lake, Hawes Water.

By mid-afternoon the weather has cleared so that one can actually distinguish clouds from the rest of the sky. I meet two women who have been looking at a golden eagle's nest through a telescope that they've lugged up from their car. It's an interminable walk along the Hawes reservoir towards Bampton where I'm staying. This body of water has been artificially created. A community was flooded and the women tell me that, in times of drought, the church steeple in the sunken village reappears.

That evening we meet a Dutch couple in the pub where we're staying at Bampton Grange. He makes truck signs and she etches. They do the Coast-to-Coast every spring. We order Westmoreland pie for dinner, it's a nice combination of turkey and ham. Not much sleep in this village though, because the church bells across the street ring every quarter hour all night. I guess the locals accept it as New Yorkers do car alarms.

Day Six—Bampton Grange through Shap to Orton-9 miles . . .
My feet are soaking from the dew before I'm through the first stile. Then in the second field of the day I meet an obnoxious bull. This is my opportunity to use the trick with my index fingers, pointed like Paul Hogan does in the Crocodile Dundee movie. It works for me too, but the bull is probably tame, or else he's slow witted and sated with so many cows to service.

I try to find a short cut down to the road at Shap Abbey, but I end up wedged under crags on an animal track. It brings me to a crevice only big enough for a sheep shelter. It's extremely awkward backing out of this while chanting: *"Old MacDonald had a farm. Ee eye ee eye o."*

At Shap, in a fish and chip shop I ask for some newspaper for my boots. While I'm eating lunch the shop owner slaps her small son for inserting a sharp knife into the plastic seat material of one of the cafeteria chairs. A cyclist comes in. He's on a charity run and the shop owner marks a score card to show that he's passed through Shap. Hey, why didn't I think of that? A Hike for the Hungry and Homeless, with Money for Miles! I could have raised big bucks in New York. Ah, well, I'll have to do the walk again!

Now it's an easy path over a railway then across a bridge over the Motorway. Seeing the six lanes of shiny speeding metal, I get a noisy fleeting reminder of the other world. On the far side of the highway there's a confusing mosaic of stone walls and fields ahead of me. The landmarks on the map seem to fit the way I'm going, but on rounding a hill I see the Motorway again. It should have been miles away from me by this time. Lost again.

Fortunately I meet a military-looking man, with leather shoulder patches on his olive green sweater. He's walking his dog and he points me in the right direction for Orton.

At the only pub I find Rosy ensconced. She has every British newspaper in print spread out around her. We stroll to a fascinating 13th century church. Inside there's a charity list from 1861 painted on a wooden wall panel. Lots of community help for the poor in those days. We investigate the bell tower with all the ropes hanging down, and diagrams of pull sequences for the different tunes. Suddenly the bells peal out. Rosy is scared that I've caused this, but it's the quarter hour ringing on an automatic timer.

In the village we find the Kennedy Chocolate Company, a sophisticated rural treat and they're generous with samples. We're told that their chocolates are used on the Concorde and in several royal households. I send some to my sister up in Edinburgh. We meet the Dutch couple again in the pub and commiserate over the cheapness of the management of this hostelry. You have to put a one pound coin in a slot for just an hour of network TV.

Day Seven—Orton to Kirkby Stephen-13 miles . . . Where we stay becomes as important as the walk itself. There's a wide variety of accommodations, and as they are pre-booked we have no choice. But we hear about other places, better and worse from the people we meet along the way. A fluid social life develops at the pubs and lunch places with other walkers on similar schedules. There are snippets of comments, and quirky characters observed ad hoc:

"Everyone knows Maureen, with her pink umbrella and plastic bags."

"What about those Canadians? Did you see the size of the backpack the old guy's toting?"

"Have you come across the Scots redhead? She's got three blokes in tow. She organizes question games at every stop for them and anyone who'll listen! One that I heard was that you had to guess the advice given to someone who writes into one of those lonely-hearts newspaper columns. 'I am a wealthy widower who has met...' that sort of thing."

We don't take the highlighted route today. Rosy is walking with me and we see on the map that we can keep to the roads. She tries different footwear and in the afternoon she gets blisters. It's due to the shoe changes, the road surface or the distance.

"*There were rats, rats, rats, rats as big as cats, In the stores, in the stores . . .*" Everything rhyming that we can think of goes into that old Boy Scout song today.

Anyway, Rosy lasts until Soulby. It's a village that looks big enough to support commerce, but there is no shop and no pub. We decide that Rosy will hitchhike to the B&B. It turns out that she doesn't need to lift her thumb more than once because a van from an old folks' recreation center stops. I tease her about the appropriateness of the transport. So she rides, and I walk, into Kirkby Stephen and through to the hamlet of Hartley, another mile.

This B&B is owned and operated by the couple who run the Packhorse service that has moved our bags and booked our beds. I have a chance to suggest improvements to their service. These ideas are not received with good grace. They charge a lot of money for the conveniences they provide, and they're not particularly flexible.

Their own accommodation is not one of the best of our Coast-to-Coast bookings. They operate a relatively primitive B&B. There's no wash basin in the room and the beds are lumpy. The next morning, our host, Mr. Bowman is snotty about providing breakfast after 7:30am. "You were told!" he retorts when we protest at 8:15am that we didn't know about his ridiculous meal time rule. He seems to believe that the customers will be so impressed by the Packhorse business niche that they won't mind discomfort.

But Mrs. Bowman's recommendation of the King Arms for dinner was brilliant. A great meal but then a cold walk back to Hartley.

Day Eight—Kirkby Stephen to Thwaite-12 miles . . . I'm walking alone today, but soon I come alongside someone who is going surprisingly fast for a stocky short-legged sixtyish woman. It's Maureen, whom several people along the way have mentioned as a role model. She's carrying *all* her gear for the fifteen-day trek. Her thighs and shoulders are festooned with plastic bags, and she's toting a frilly edged pink umbrella.

Inevitably on a popular trail you'll come alongside someone going in the same direction, and you decide whether you want to slow down and chat or pass with a wave and a "good morning." The protocol of joining up with another walker is that you don't actually ask if you can walk with someone. You're kind of doing that anyway. But if you find that you're both going at more or less the same pace, then the joining up evolves. You introduce yourself and maybe swap life stories. There's no feeling of rejection when either person wants to take a longer break, and the important thing is not to invade anyone's contemplative space. So you walk on alone if you feel like it, because as the villages are so tiny and the tea/beer opportunities so few and far between, you know you're probably going to meet up later.

Today I have serial join-ups. After Maureen stops to soak her feet, I come across Mac, a taciturn machine tool worker from Nottingham. A few miles further on, there's Mike who's aiming for youth hostels instead of pubs. He's done the Coast-to-Coast four times already, with different family members. He asks if I've seen Maureen, and he seems relieved to hear that she's far behind. She *is* a bit intense.

The highest point today is the Nine Standards peak. The weather is good so I can see it clearly. By now I've left the Lake District and I've come into the Dales. This is the area where they filmed "All Creatures Great and Small." It was a TV show about a veterinarian. The words of the title are from a children's hymn. It was my mantra a few days ago and now I'm fixated on the schoolboy parody:

"All things bright and beautiful, all creatures grunt and smell."

Rosy is waiting at Whitehead's Guest House at Thwaite. In the dining room we meet a Baptist church outing from Newcastle. They come every year for a few days of walks in the Dales. There don't seem to be any Yanks up in this part of England so Rosy the New Yorker gets all the questions about the American stuff they see on the telly.

We also meet a couple, Jack and Ethel, who come to Thwaite from London at the same time each year because they had their honeymoon here. They're not connected with the church group from Newcastle, but their visit coincides with the Baptists every year. Each year Jack teases the Baptist leader and tries to get him drunk. This time he succeeds. It's sad because then we get the leader's garrulous monologue about the way he organizes his walks with the train schedules. He's trying to be so precise, and the Baptist ladies look upset when he slurs his words.

They have a fixed menu here at Whitehead's: cod, whether you like it or not.

Day Nine—Thwaite to Reeth-11 miles . . . After Rosy has gone off with the luggage, I meet some local teachers who tell me that the prettiest walk today will be along the Swale River. My strip map shows a path over the mountain, which would be following Wainwright's route. I'm opting for the low road along the river, so I buy a different map of the Dales area and set off towards the village of Muker.

However small, all these villages have a Public Hall, a Literary Institute, and a Methodist Chapel. The development beyond basic agriculture hereabouts came with the need for raw materials during the Industrial Revolution. The hills were full of iron ore, lead and coal. Queen Victoria adored black jewelry, so jet was mined here too.

The industrialists of the time sponsored the public buildings, maybe with the guilty aim of uplifting the lives of their workers. Now many of these imposing brick and stone structures have been tastefully converted to homes. Nothing much happens in these villages now, so many residents are retired or commute to the cities. But they've been human settlements for so long that each and every one of them has a story to discover. One place has the Bed and Breakfast haunted by a naked, well-hung monk, another has the pub where a fleeing king had his last fling before capture.

This is the best day yet for flowers. As far as the eye can see, there are whole fields of buttercups and woods carpeted with bluebells.

Near the Swale River there are acres of rabbit kingdoms, with a thousand baby bunnies scampering about. It smells a bit rank though, and there are so many holes that I almost twist my ankle.

"*Steady the Buffs!*" as my military Uncle Tom used to say. It was his regimental mantra during the desert battles against Rommel.

The teachers who'd suggested the riverside path have driven to Muker and they invite me to linger for coffee. They're in no rush and they bombard me with questions about the USA. Is it really like a book they've just enjoyed, Bill Bryson's *The Lost Continent*? I suggest Jonathan Raban and some other travel authors I've enjoyed.

In the pub at lunch everyone's talking about a race over the mountain paths. I assume that they are referring to cyclists, as I've seen so many, but when I get to Reeth I meet the winner of the men's section of a local marathon. A mountain marathon, not on a bike. It exhausts me to think of *racing* through this countryside. The winner looks like a greyhound and he's done the 26 miles in 3 hours. We talk about the London and New York races, and he says that "darkies" shouldn't be permitted to compete in these events because they live at such high altitudes in Africa. He says that it's not fair because they've got bigger lungs.

We're staying with Mrs. Crawford, who's very welcoming. She's very chic and elegant too, except for the profusion of hair flowing out of her armpits. There is a good little library in the bedroom here where Mrs. C. lets me borrow two of George Melly's three autobiographies. I'll later send them back with some saltwater taffy. She remembers the taste of it from a vacation in Atlantic City.

Rosy and I are running out of cash and we have to find an ATM soon. Reeth's a pretty place, plenty of accommodations and pubs, but there's no bank. We have a decent meal at the Buck Hotel. It has the only restaurant that takes Visa.

Day Ten—Reeth to Richmond–10 1/2 miles... The first part of my morning is through outrageously beautiful buttercup fields. It's a lowland walk today. The villages look big enough to support commerce but have no shops or cafes. Finally, at Marske, I see a sign: "Refreshments—in aid of the Church Repair Fund. Go 150 yards to the right." It's Sunday and this is church service time, so the refreshment house owners are probably in church praying for a new roof. Their grandchildren are dispensing the scones. A number of hikers stop for a snack, and the children keep mixing up the orders. Butter is smeared on the teacups and there's great jollity all round.

The rest of the way into Richmond is through dense woodland and I arrive in the town at 2pm. It's a big urban center and I have no town map. Luckily, I meet someone who knows the streets so that I can find the B&B.

I meet Rosy who has already looked round the town center and found an ATM. She says it didn't work at first when she tried it. But then it disgorged cash when she chose the instructions in German. It must be the fact that, in letters, her PIN spells 'heil'.

Richmond Castle is fascinating. Alain of Brittany had quite a set up here after the Norman Conquest. For that time, it must have been a very elaborate household. Later, much later, Lord Baden-Powell, who became the founder of the Boy Scouts, was the local military commander. I wonder if he buggered any subalterns here. During both World Wars conscientious objectors were imprisoned in the castle. *"Onward, Christian soldiers..."* as we walk around the castle grounds.

It's a standard, efficient B&B tonight. The walkers are talking about the arduous day ahead. It's the longest one, but by now I feel fit for almost anything. We find excellent French cuisine at a tiny bistro in the town.

Day Eleven—Richmond to Ingleby Cross-23 miles... Rosy wants to check out some antique shops and I take the main road for 4 miles to save time. There's no sidewalk. Unfortunately this means hassling with commuters into Richmond. Housewives driving Range Rovers carrying pigtailed girls in school uniforms follow them. I stick out my tongue at them as they pass, swooshing mud on me.

I join the Wainwright trail at Catterick. As it's still early, the trail is very dewy through the fields. Then I have a long stretch on quiet back roads. I'm going very fast, but I'm slightly knackered by the time I get to the pub at Darby Wiske. The dry socks that I change into are a welcome relief. Here we go, Christmas carol parody mantra: *"While shepherds washed their socks by night..."*

There's quite a crowd of walkers here that I've met before. Martin, whose computer was stolen before he came on holiday, makes me think that I'll get a Zipdrive to back up my computer files when I'm back in the real world. Bernie owns a Toyota dealership and we discuss an idea I have for an on-line used car price directory. (Oh, Craig, you prescient person.)

The landlord of the pub has a guest book and he seems to have the best informal statistics on how many people really take the Coast-to-Coast walk. The road past his pub is the only way through this area. Additionally, his is the only place that you come across all day for food, drink, and a toilet. I sign the guest book and notice that twelve people have already passed through here just today.

I stick with Martin and Bernie all afternoon, even when they stop to brew tea.

At Ingleby Cross I meet Rosy at Monks House which is owned by Mrs. Backhouse. Inside it's a visual outrage. There are stuffed, ceramic, knitted, woven mice on every surface. Other collections abound. Horse brasses and post cards mingle with the mice. This cluttered-up, classic building dates from 1300 AD. Ah, well, maybe the monk was a packrat too.

Mrs. Backhouse provides a great bed, the firmest we've had. We have a fun dinner at the Blue Bell Inn. The whole crowd is there, with stories to swap and exploits to share. We're at a table with Kevin and Christine from Burnley. He's a plumber and she works in a bookshop. He organizes an annual bike race down the length of the British Isles for charity and he tells us hilarious tales about collecting money for it. Christine's accent reminds me of a favorite aunt who lived in a town near Burnley.

Rosy and I sleep blissfully on that super firm mattress and Mrs. Backhouse features twelve different marmalades at breakfast.

Day Twelve—Ingleby Cross to Urra Bilsdale-14 miles... It's a cloudy morning and my big debate is whether to wear long or short pants. I decide that it will be cold up on the moors and I wear long pants. I realize that this was a bad decision when I get up on the moor and it starts to pour with rain. On with the poncho. But I'm weighed down by sopping long pants instead of just having wet legs.

Soon I'm ready for a break. The map shows a building up here somewhere, but I walk a couple of hours without coming across even a sheep shelter. The mantra of the day is *"Ten green bottles"*—grimly chanted.

Coming over the brow of a hill I see cars parked on a rectangle of asphalt. It's in the middle of nowhere but there's a black ribbon of road leading to it. Then I realize that a chimney is poking out of the grass on the hill. I've found a cafe in a cave. I climb down to the entrance and find the place chock-a-block with smelly walkers, all steaming off the rain.

They call out a welcome to me, "Here comes the yellow monk." My poncho is sensibly tied up with Rosy's silken rope. I will manage to leave it at the next B& B, a lamented loss.

Within minutes of leaving the cafe, my clothes have dried out from the wind. The next people I encounter are a group of child cyclists. They're all black or brown skinned, wearing beige dungarees. They're riding with two gung-ho leaders who blow their whistles for me to get out of their way. Maybe it's some sort of English Fresh Air Fund.

Then there are lots of conifer plantations. I detour around the last mini mountain of the day. It's called Wainstones. Wow! Odd ancient rock formations Wow! Pass, I'm getting blasé about antiquity.

Instead of the climb, I come down the road through a glorious bluebell wood. But when I think that I should be reaching my destination for the day, the only road sign is confusing. Then I remember something about a disused mailbox that our fusspot hostess had mentioned over breakfast. We'd been discussing our route for the day. Thank you, Mrs. Backhouse, for the important road clue you gave me. I finally find Maltkiln House and our hosts, Mr. and Mrs. Broad.

Before getting there, I'm aware of some very noisy sheep. A field to my right is practically wall to wall with animals. Later I hear from Mr. Broad that his neighbor, who is the owner of the sheep has three times the legal density of animals in his field. There is some sort of complicated European Common Market agricultural fiddling going on.

Hey, this is the best B&B yet. We have a tasteful room with no screaming color and design clashes. The bathroom is state of the art, and the host family is interesting, articulate and friendly. Rosy has already had a tour of the farm, met the prize pet pig, and has Mr. Broad's e-mail address. They're way off the beaten track and cater only to walkers. These generous folks serve us sherry before dinner, then tons of food, a big selection of wines and powerful ale called Double Maxim.

We've a great crowd, Kevin and Christine from Burnley, Gary, a police chief from Surrey and his wife Jane, and the young honeymoon couple whom we've seen along the way. They were cuddling together up on the moor. There is also Mr. Whitlock who'd retired from the Forestry Commission. He's full of technical tree knowledge that we tap when we engage him in conversation.

Gary is the one who gets a post card from his brother at every stop along the way. The cards are waiting for him wherever he arrives for the night. Each one has questions that he must answer about the local area. Then he must mail it back to his brother from that area. It proves that Gary has been there. Now he's retaliating. He's making one up to send back to test his brother's knowledge. We all dream up some dumb thing about beer, bullets, and Boers using the words Double Maxim.

Mr. Whitlock has had too much beer and he goes to bed. Saying goodnight he mildly complains about sleeping alone in the room belonging to the Broad's absent daughter. He giggles that he wouldn't mind if the daughter were there, and we all chorus, "Oh, Mr. Whitlock!" in mock shock.

Day Thirteen—Urra Bilsdale to Blakey-8 miles . . . Mr. Broad's recommended path takes us back west some way, but soon we pick up the Cleveland Way that will join up with the Coast-to-Coast trail. It's windy and Rosy is not wearing enough layers. She wears my extra socks for gloves. We're able to keep up a fast pace through the featureless moors because there is nothing to linger for. Our first shelter is in a grouse butt which shooters use. For a break it's very cozy, then later we find a mini quarry on the lee side of a bluff away from the wind.

"*Clippety cloppety, jiggery pokery.*" My mantra for the day is from George Starbuck, a poet who has nothing to do with coffee.

Most of this day's walk is on a flat, cinder track of an abandoned mine railway which was laid through the moors a hundred and fifty years ago. We see old iron mines, jet mines, and rusted machinery. All moors, all day. There is neither pub, nor cafe, nor village until we see the Lion Inn. This is about as isolated as one can get in England. There's just the big pub and something called the High Blakey House on the other side of the road. This is our place for the night. It's a strangely shaped house, but an efficient B&B, and there's good food with the usual group of walkers across at the pub where they're staying.

Day Fourteen—Blakey to Egton Bridge-10 miles . . . There aren't many trees up here, but when I see some after a cool walk over the moor I realize that the white hawthorn has blossomed overnight. I think of holly, then Christmas, and I break into: *"Jingle Bells, Batman smells, Robin laid an egg."*

I meet Kevin and Christine brewing up some tea. So many of the English walkers carry Primus stoves, Sterno, or something to make the water hot for their tea en route. With milk and sugar, properly stewed, and no bloody teabags, thank you.

The next village is Eskdale. It's very pretty, like Swaledale a few days back. There's a splendid balmy walk through the woods to Egton Bridge. We're staying in the Horseshoe Hotel. There are gigantic trees in the garden—chestnut, sequoia pine and laburnum with its droopy bright yellow blossoms like lupins. It's been a warm day with no clouds.

The next day is the last one, ending on the East Coast. At dinner that night the walkers are talking about the logistics of getting home. Some will be picked up and others have to catch a train. We've all told our respective life stories and tonight we all get the chance to tell all the old jokes that only our spouses have heard before.

The Bowmans from Packhorse have told Rosy today that a British TV film crew is making a movie about Coast-to-Coast walkers and the Packhorse service. Christine promises to tape it for us and send it at Christmas. Meeting all these people has been purely ad hoc, but tomorrow everyone will diverge, so we become a bit maudlin. We all make promises to swap photos and diaries, but this is before everyone has e-mail and digital images so you don't hold your breath about it happening.

Day Fifteen—Egton Bridge to Robin Hood's Bay-18 miles . . .

I set off at a furious pace, following a horse down a lane. Actually, I'm following a woman with waistlength blonde hair, on a horse down a lane. She's clothed, but I'm thinking Lady Godiva. She's riding faster than I walk though, and then she turns off somewhere at the end of the lane. This old track had been a toll road even into the 1940's and there's a plaque on a fencepost describing its operation.

I can hear a steam engine over the hill. As we lived near a railway when I was a kid, it's very evocative. Grosmont, around the next bend in the road, is a village with a restored station for the tourist steam railway.

There's a fierce hill climb up out of Grosmont. It's a 1 in 3 gradient, which means you move one foot up for every three feet forward. That's a first gear hill for any vehicle, and it's a killer for me. You don't anticipate these things on the map because walls and other features often diffuse the tight gradient lines. Up onto the moor I meet two couples again that I'd seen a week ago. They're doing the walk with a dog, a golden Labrador who loves rolling in the heather. Then I meet a few other people but I don't want to chat today and I press ahead.

"*On Ilkley moor bar t'at . . .*" It's a mournful dirge, my mantra today. The song is all about a lovelorn man who caught his death of cold by going out on the moor without his hat.

I assume that I'll find a pub or a teashop in Little Beck, but there's nothing. I chat with a couple who are considering buying a good-looking Victorian five-bedroom house. I suggest the commercial possibilities of a B&B and tearoom to them because of the strategic location of the house. They're up from London looking for a weekend retreat. My idea is obviously irrelevant to them, but at least they listen politely.

On through the forest I trudge. One of the remarkable sights in this forest is a hermit's cave. It's not a cave in the hillside. It's a gigantic freestanding boulder with the dwelling carved into it. It has an arched doorway and within there's a room about eight cubic feet with a stone bench hollowed out of the rock walls. Over the doorway, 1790 has been elegantly etched. This place gets my imagination going, thinking about a succession of imbeciles straining their hearts and hacking their way into this piece of the planet.

After a series of waterfalls I take what I hope is a short cut. It's a path that is unmarked on the map. I'm probably following animal spoors, and I haven't learned my lesson from other days. But, what d'you know, I get lucky and, coming out of the woods I find myself standing on a road that's not on my map. A few yards down this mystery road, I meet other Coast-to-Coast folks just at the right moment for directions.

Even though I've been doing this for fifteen days my feet are killing me when I finally find a pub at 2pm in Hawsker. I take the boots off, quaff a pint and a half in no time at all, and even though it's "afterhours," the landlord makes me an egg and cheese sandwich. What a Prince! Who says that the culture of service is dead in the United Kingdom?

Nearly there now, only a few miles more!

I can glimpse the coastline now. It's beautiful; a sight for sore eyes, feet, muscles, et cetera. There are some holiday caravan sites to navigate through in order to get to the Cliff walk. Then my last two dramatic miles are along the rim, around the curve of the Bay and down into the village.

It's a grand finish, and Rosy is the most welcome sight of all when I come down the hill to the last B&B and the eastern seashore.